What do you get when you combine a native New Yorker, church planter, husband, father, and practitioner in renowned Uptown, New York City? The answer is in your hand! In *Mi Casa Uptown: Learning to Love Again*, you'll discover firsthand learnings on what it means to be a true disciple in an ever-changing urban context. In this book, Rich gives away the recipe on how to foster authentic Christ-centered community: plant roots, make homes, build families, love neighbors, trust Jesus, and die well. This book should be required reading in every church-planting movement. I am grateful for Rich and the entire Christ Crucified Fellowship (CCF) family as they faithfully make much of Jesus—in the heights and beyond!

—Ralph Castillo, teaching pastor
of Christ Tabernacle

You can't truly love a city unless you love the people. Many people have expressed their love for New York, yet forsake the very people who've called it home their entire life! In *Mi Casa Uptown*, Pastor Rich Pérez brings balance to the conversation by expressing love for his God, city, and the people who've intersected their life with his. Hear his heart and emulate it in your city for God's glory.

—D. A. Horton, pastor of Reach Church
and author of *Bound to Be Free*

In this heartfelt incarnational memoir, Pérez unpacks a fresh and needed gospel voice for city and urban ministry. He communicates about the Empire State in the neighborhood of Washington Heights in a way that makes it approachable. Read this work and be inspired to fill where God has sent you with new redemptive stories.

—Eric M. Mason, lead pastor of Epiphany Fellowship and author of *Unleashed: Being Conformed to the Image of Christ*

Regardless of your faith, this book will stimulate and challenge your thinking. Rich takes you on an intimate tour of self that at times puts you in the position of the protagonist. He effortlessly weaves correlations between love, Jesus, and community, and cocoons you in a quilt of reflection. From my favorite childhood memory to my present life experiences, this book forces you to rethink your perspective about all things life.

—Belissa Savery, director of Client Partnerships for Cine Latino

Mi Casa Uptown is a refreshing reexamination of the callous assumptions we attach to the city, and how life and beauty can still be found there despite those assumptions.

—B. J. Thompson, executive director and founder of Build a Better Us

America is returning to cities to live, and many never left. For those who love the city and who love Jesus, this will be an incredibly challenging and deeply moving read. For those not sure about Jesus, this will be a surprising encounter—not with religion, but with love. And love can change everything!

—John Avant, senior pastor of
First Baptist Concord, Knoxville, Tennessee

I love the way that Rich makes the ordinary seem so exciting and fulfilling. He reminds me that my ordinary life is filled with so many opportunities for greatness that we're oblivious to. Throughout this book, Rich, almost like a magician, pulls so much meaning and wonder out of what seems to be so mundane. As long as I've known Rich, I've known of his love for his city, his family, his neighborhood, and most important, his God—and it's contagious. I'm so grateful that he actually took the time to unpack all of his loves in one place so anyone who picks this up can catch some of what he has. Your family, your faith, and your neighborhood will be better off if any of this sticks.

—John Onwuchekwa, lead pastor of
Cornerstone Church, Atlanta, Georgia

After living and pastoring in New York City for nine years, one of my biggest regrets is not spending more time with Rich Pérez. He loves his city, not in a romantic way, but in a real and sacrificial way. His words are refreshing and challenging, inspiring us to plant ourselves and live invested in the places we inhabit, for the glory of God and good of neighbor.

—JR Vassar, pastor and author of *Glory Hunger: God, the Gospel* and *Our Quest for Something More*

This is a wonderful expression of love for family, community, and Christ. It's nostalgic for some, enlightening for others, and challenging for all.

—David Ham, pastor of evangelism at Times Square Church, New York City

Rich is still that same hospitable man who would offer his apartment in a split second to anyone in need. No matter how similar or different your life experiences may be, my hope is that as you read *Mi Casa Uptown*, you would be challenged and inspired by Rich's journey.

—Andy Mineo, recording artist and friend

Pérez delivers an unbelievably rich and compelling narrative about life in New York City that is hidden from the world because the storytellers are from the dominant culture. The redemptive story of the gospel is woven into this story in rich layers that will inspire readers to love God and love their neighbors in their own communities. In *Mi Casa Uptown*, New York City and the gospel come to life in ways that encourage us all to seek first the kingdom.

—Anthony B. Bradley, PhD., associate professor of Religious Studies at The King's College, New York, New York

MI CASA
UPTOWN

MI CASA UPTOWN

LEARNING TO LOVE AGAIN

RICH PÉREZ

B&H
PUBLISHING GROUP

NASHVILLE, TENNESSEE

Published by B&H Publishing Group
Nashville, Tennessee

Dewey Decimal Classification: 152.4
Subject Heading: LOVE \ EMOTIONS \ PREJUDICES

Designer: Adalis Martinez
Photo: Ray Neutron
Illustrator: RJ Vergara

1 2 3 4 5 6 7 • 21 20 19 18 17

Dedication

"*Tú*"

I remember it as if it happened yesterday. "Tú," sung by Juan Luis Guerra, was one of my mom's favorite songs to dance to. The DJ at my wedding called us up for the last dance, and despite the fact that she was physically struggling, she wasn't going to pass up the moment—a moment that only later we'd realize we wouldn't get back. My mom's commitment to work, serve, teach, lead, and inspire anyone in her path was infectious. And that night was no different.

Mi Casa Uptown is dedicated not only to my mom's legacy, but to every immigrant who moves their family to an unfamiliar land with a dream all too familiar. Thank you. Your commitments, efforts, sacrifices, long hours, overnights, broken English, odd jobs, native tongue, food—everything—has been nothing but inspiring to your children, their children, and the work and purpose with which they now live. You are the real heroes, even if few honor you. *Gracias, Papi y Mami.*

Mi Casa Uptown is dedicated to my wife, Anna. You've been nothing but incredible, not only through the writing process, but since we first met in the fitting room at the Gap over fourteen years ago. I commit to never leave you nor stop pursuing you. For where you go I will go, and where you stand I will stand. Your family shall be my family, and your God my God. Where you die I will die, and there will I be buried. May the Lord do so to me and more also if anything but death parts me from you.

Finally, *Mi Casa Uptown* is dedicated to my son, Josiah. My little superhero, Jo "Whadoyaknow." In our world, people find it hard to be themselves. God has used you to inspire me to be me. The forgiven, made-new, and Spirit-empowered me. You're an incredible little dude, brighter than you sometimes know. You are the single greatest reason in this life I labored writing this book, building our home, investing in this community, leaving this legacy. No matter what life throws your way (because it will, and it throws hard!), Jesus made sure that there's always a place to take those things. Just before you think the light is swallowed up by darkness; just before you think evil wins; just before you think the fire is put out by the cold—that's when the light explodes everywhere. That's when good stands tall with evil under foot. That's when the fire spreads, creating passion and strength to believe again. I hope that the life of this book is something you experience with me before anyone else. I hope that the life of this book inspires you to find Jesus in the smallest things as much as in the biggest; in the familiar as much as in the unfamiliar; in all the places you travel, but even more, in your home, *tu casa*. Love you, buddy.

About the Author

Through a variety of speaking experiences, Rich Pérez has grown into a unique storyteller and thought-leader in faith, family, the arts, and the Hispanic-American experience. In 2011 Rich and his family led a team of friends into his hometown neighborhood (Washington Heights) and started a church that would embrace the very values with which they lived. Rich is the lead pastor of Christ Crucified Fellowship in New York City, where he lives with his wife and kids.

Contents

La Bienvenida: **Bustelo** in My Cup Again

by Andy Mineo

I blew it. I missed my alarm clock on the single most important day on the job as resident assistant—move-in day. "Andy, are you in there?!" I heard my boss yell through the door as he pounded on it. "I swear, if you're asleep, you're fired!" As a broke college student living in New York City, the only way I could afford my dorm room was by being an RA, because they got free housing in return for working for the school. Now that my job was gone, and my housing provision with it, I had two weeks to get out of the dorms. I was heading toward homelessness, and I didn't know what to do.

So I called a friend of mine who had just moved back to New York from Bible college—Rich Pérez.

Rich and I used to serve together in a ministry called TRUCE, Nicky Cruz Outreach. We would travel the world using our talents as artists to share our faith in some of the most desperate and violent communities. In case you didn't know, Rich once had a rap career! And don't let the *pastor* title fool you—he still might spit a few bars every now and then.

Anyway, back to the story. I called Rich and explained to him how I had lost my job and apartment. I asked if he had any leads on places I could rent on a college-student budget. Almost without hesitation, he said, "Bro, just come stay with us." By *us* he meant him, his wife, Anna, and their two-year-old son, Josiah. We've all heard the famous Spanish phrase *Mi casa es su casa*, which means "My house is your house." I thought to myself, *This dude really takes that seriously!*

Two weeks later, I was moving an air mattress and trash bags full of my clothes into Josiah's room. At that point, Rich wasn't a pastor. He was working at Trump SoHo, an upscale hotel where rich people and celebrities liked to stay. Dinners together, after a long day of work for Rich, would be filled with questions. "So did Chris Brown stay there this week?" "You saw Will Smith in the bathroom?!" "Wait, you room serviced Nas an order of bacon and talked to him about *Illmatic*?!" When we weren't talking about the interesting celebrities Rich was running into at work, we talked about Uptown and the day when his true passion and vision as a church planter and pastor would be realized. In that cramped, two-bedroom apartment, we would dream dreams and make plans about what a church in that neighborhood could look like. We dreamed about a young, vibrant, urban church that valued sound theology, fostered strong community, welcomed the unchurched, and served people fearlessly.

After four months with the Pérez family, I found an apartment with a handful of friends who were eager to be part of the vision for this church. We started meeting in my new apartment on Sundays before we officially launched.

Fast-forward five years, and Rich is now my pastor. But not only mine—he is the lead pastor of Christ Crucified Fellowship in uptown Manhattan. Hundreds of people gather weekly to hear him share stories of life, faith, and hope from his unique perspective. Rich is well loved and respected locally and nationally, as an effective communicator and visionary. But his public recognition is not why I recommend this book to you.

I recommend this book to you because of who Rich is in private.

Some say, "If you want to know how great a man is, ask his wife." In other words, ask the people who really know him, the people who see him when the mask is off. I can say without any hesitation that Rich is respected and loved by those closest to him as a man of thought, integrity, and honor. As long as I have known him, Rich has been a seeker of truth, eager to find ways to live out his Christianity more faithfully. Rich is still that same hospitable man who would offer his apartment in a split second to anyone in need. No matter how similar or different your life experiences may be, my hope is that as you read *Mi Casa Uptown* you will be challenged and inspired by Rich's journey.

They say the best part of leaving New York is coming back, so I'ma live and leave it all on my legal pads. Hopefully I make tracks for you to follow; if hallowed be Thy name then how do I live the same?

—Rich Pérez, from *Coming Home*

Familiarity Breeds
. . . Love?

As a child I believed that my neighborhood was the world. Not in the sense that it meant the world to me—although I loved it—but it was literally all I knew. In my mind, there wasn't much outside of my neighborhood. Lin-Manuel, who wrote and starred in my favorite Broadway show, *In the Heights*, put it perfectly for me: "I used to think we lived at the top of the world, when the world was just a subway map . . . I used to think the Bronx was a place in the sky, when the world was just a subway map . . ."[1] I looked at the subway map every time we traveled on the train, and mostly I saw Uptown—and a portion of the Bronx, of course. But on the map between the Bronx and my neighborhood was a misty, light blue space, which in my young and imaginative mind was sky, not water. I know that seems naive, but often that's what children are—naive. I knew places like Brooklyn and Queens were real, but to my little mind, they seemed like a world away. I think even now, as an adult, I still somewhat believe that.

As far back as I can remember, that was my childhood. Family lived here. My friends were here. School was here. My countless dreams to conquer the world came from this place (and, of course, from my *Pinky and the Brain* fascination).

On one hand, that way of thinking is naive and can often isolate us from the rest of the world. It can keep us from exploring and discovering the beauty that exists in every corner of the world. But we also run the risk of unintentionally living out that old saying, *familiarity breeds contempt*.

On the other hand, there's something equally special and rewarding in the mind-set that pursues familiarity. It inspires locality. It inspires intentional presence. It inspires sticking around long enough. Long enough for what? Long enough for, well . . . anything. Most of us don't often see things change, because we don't commit to the process that change requires. Our neighborhoods and cities would greatly benefit from the mind-set that pursues and values familiarity.

Extensive knowledge of, or close association with, people or things often leads to a loss of respect for them. That old saying—familiarity breeds contempt—is based on the idea that if we stick around long enough to experience the *little* good, the *hopelessly* bad, and the *really* ugly of people or things, we won't like what we see and we'll decide we need to run in the opposite direction. Or perhaps worse, some of us will make familiar people or things pay for having so *little* good but so *much* bad, and for being *really* ugly. We'll hold a grudge, speak ill of them, or hold them at a distance until we feel they've earned the right to be close again. Simply put, we objectify people whom we think we've figured out. And there's no question that we're all guilty of it.

Sometimes we feel contempt for people and view them as worthless or beneath us as a result of knowing too much about them or getting too close to them. But what if we flipped that on its head? What if instead of breeding contempt, familiarity resulted in love—a sort of out-of-this-world kind of love? What if every new experience of a person or place caused us to gain respect instead of lose it? What if every new thing we learned about a person or place didn't push us away but made us lean in and draw closer? What if the ugly things we see in each other, and in the places we're from, didn't lead us to close one another off but instead led us to confront the ugliness, embrace it, and help transform it? What if our weaknesses didn't divide us but instead united us with much greater passion?

Subway map at Dyckman Street in the train station.

It's a Love/Hate Thing

Maybe this childhood memory can help illustrate what I mean. Saturday mornings were incredible when I was growing up. They really were. Ask any kid who grew up in my neighborhood and most of them would share similar stories.

Eran la siete de la mañana
y uno por uno al matadero
pues cada cual tiene su precio
buscando visa para un sueño[2]

Juan Luis Guerra was up earlier than me on most Saturdays. In fact, I often woke up to him singing and my dad making *farina* in the unbelievably small corner of our kitchen where the stove was. My mom, swaying from side to side to *"Buscando Visa,"* vacuumed the living room. And not too long after my teenaged butt rolled out of bed, I heard my mom utter a few words that now as an adult I miss hearing: *"Richa! ve a la panadería y compra uno cuanto panes."* Going to Kenny's Bakery on Dyckman Street meant so much more than just going to any bakery to grab bread. Those seemingly insignificant bread runs were important because they meant we would all sit and enjoy breakfast together. They etched in me a deep sense of family and helped me see that the greatest assets I'll ever have are moments with people—not moments with things. Of course, my siblings and I often took that for granted, just as every teenager does.

But among those great experiences were several difficult ones. One in particular involved me waking up early on a Saturday morning, running to the bakery, eating breakfast, and then running outside to play some basketball. The hoop was just across the street. My dad would grab a pillow from the couch and lay it on the windowsill to keep his forearms from being bruised or scratched as he watched out the window. I always found something interesting about my dad doing that. He wanted to keep an eye on us, but he did that even when we weren't outside. It was a sort of neighborhood-watch quirk he had. He kept up with the different things happening on the block.

Anyway, I ran outside to play ball. There was only one kid, Johnny, at the court shooting around. I knew him from around the way, and I knew he was good—but not good enough to beat me. I was pretty good! (I like to think that I still am.) I also knew that Johnny had a temper, so playing a one-on-one with him, knowing that I would probably beat him, wasn't a good idea, but I did it anyway. As the game picked up, things got heated and a crowd gathered around us. It was game point. Next basket would win, and I had possession. I made a couple of moves, faked Johnny left to right, and took a fifteen-foot jump shot. Remember when I said I was good? I wasn't kidding. The shot was all net!

I never doubted winning the game. What I did have doubts about was Johnny's reaction. He was upset, and the crowd around us egged him on, which didn't help. Johnny walked right up to me and, without any hesitation, punched me right in the face. The punch wasn't a total surprise, but in my best Kevin Hart impersonation, "I wasn't ready!" I curled up a bit while everyone waited to see what I would do. It was as if the world had gone mute for a moment. It might have been the punch to the side of my face. But then out of the silence came my dad's heavy, yet piercing, voice from the window, "*Qué tú e'pera? Dale!*" So I did. I retaliated with a fist full of frustration and pride. But ten minutes later, I was just another victim of Johnny's anger and size. He kicked my behind. I got a couple of licks in, but it was clear that Johnny had won the fight.

Here's what I realized: working hard, doing your best, or being good at something sometimes gets you punched in the face. And that's certainly not the result you would expect. But that's life, isn't it? Life is messy and out of whack. There's good, there's bad, and there's ugly. And nowadays, it's becoming apparent that there is disproportionately more bad and ugly than there is good, no matter how hard you look for the good. Even a model optimist eventually will come to realize that the lights are off more than they are on. But the key, I'm learning, is to acknowledge that we cannot avoid the mess or run from the darkness. We cannot simply travel to a place where brokenness doesn't exist. When things feel like they don't work quite the way they should, we can't just build something else and not expect the same thing to happen again, sooner or later. Where we are, there the brokenness is also. This might sound a bit brash, but only if there isn't hope.

To love our cities and neighborhoods—and the people who live in them—we can't escape our world, and we shouldn't conform to it. Instead, we should inspire it. But there's a tension in that, isn't there? There certainly is, but I think it's a helpful tension.

On the one hand, we love our cities deeply enough to challenge them in ways we believe they need to be challenged. It's like the coaches you had growing up in high school. They were so deeply invested in you that they felt like your mentors. Every team had that one player who was incredibly talented but had a devastatingly poor work ethic. The coach loved the player, and would do his best to celebrate his talent and potential, but the poor work ethic drove the coach to hate the player just as much as he loved him! He loved *and* hated the player enough to want to see him change and leave those character traits behind. Likewise, although we love our cities enough to count them worthy of change, we hate them enough to work toward that change.

G. K. Chesterton, an English poet and philosopher, describes the tension of Christian faithfulness to this world:

> No one doubts that an ordinary man can get on with this world: but we demand not strength enough to get on with it, but strength enough to get it on. Can he hate it enough to change it, and yet love it enough to think it worth changing? Can he look up at its colossal good without once feeling acquiescence? Can he look up at its colossal evil without once feeling despair? Can he, in short, be at once not only a pessimist and an optimist, but a fanatical pessimist and a fanatical optimist? Is he enough of a pagan to die for the world, and enough of a Christian to die to it? In this combination, I maintain, it is the rational optimist who fails, the irrational optimist who succeeds. He is ready to smash the whole universe for the sake of itself.[3]

Just like the invested coach, Chesterton's "irrational optimist" loves the player deeply because of his talent and potential, but hates him because of his devastatingly poor work ethic. He'll work him and work him so much that it would seem as though he's out to destroy him, when in fact he is trying to build him up.

That's how we love the city. It almost feels like a love affair, honestly. I'm sure that most of you love the places you're from. You love your city deeply, but you love even more the city that it could be. Sadly, if familiarity with our cities only breeds contempt, there will be no room for their renewal. So what will it take for familiarity to breed love, rather than contempt?

My family and friends have a motto, a guiding philosophy by which we try to live. Maybe it will help you answer that question. *Plant roots, make homes, build families, love neighbors, trust Jesus, and die well.* In other words, vision, commitment, relationships, faith, and legacy will be our biggest players in helping reshape the story told by our cities and neighborhoods. It was the story of a first-century Galilean fisherman, rabbi, and self-proclaimed God, who changed the course of my life and subsequently influenced the way I see and approach my city. The story of Jesus, as the

Bible tells it, allows familiarity to stir up love, rather than contempt.

If you've read up to this point, this is probably when you get frustrated and ask for the tab. You're ready to check out. You don't want to be preached to. You don't want to hear about religion. Or maybe you're the believer who has been inundated with Christian books, articles, and stories. But let me say this: just give it a chance. I'm not the imposing type, so you won't get that here. I'm just looking to share my story, my love for my neighborhood, and the hope I have for it—and along the way inspire faith, commitment, imagination, and hope.

So how does the story of Jesus help us travel from a place of familiarity, bypass contempt, and arrive at love?

A Fascination

The answer, I believe, is found in a simple observation in God's narrative. Throughout his time on earth, we know of only two times when Jesus wept. In John 11:35 the apostle John tells us that after the death of Lazarus, a close friend, "Jesus wept." Even if you didn't grow up in a religious culture, I'm sure you've heard that passage. It's the shortest verse in the whole Bible.

The only other occasion when Jesus weeps is found in Luke 19:41. There, Jesus, after being extravagantly welcomed into Jerusalem by the people, walks to a place where he can get a good view of the entire city of Jerusalem. "As he approached and saw the city, he wept for it."

What does this say to us? It tells us that Jesus wasn't running around crying all the time. But it also draws our attention to what Jesus' heart longs for—a city. Stephen T. Um, a Christian minister in Boston, and Justin Buzzard, a pastor in Silicon Valley, both talk about the significance of this observation. "At the center of the Christian faith stands a savior who wept over a city he loved. Jesus was emotionally involved with this city—both its beauty and brokenness deeply affected him."[4]

There's a kind of fascination and hopeful vision that ran through the veins of Jesus as he stood at the edge of the cliff looking out into the city. I like to think that the moment was similar to how I grew up as a kid in our cozy Uptown apartment. In the bitter cold of December, the heating pipes loudly hissed at us and then clapped a few times when we didn't hear them hiss. The kids stared intently at the presents, waiting for the clock to hit midnight on Christmas Eve. We felt an incredible sense of anticipation, knowing the joy that was coming.

Similarly, I imagine that in that moment, Jesus was gripped by a sense of anticipation, knowing what he would soon do for Jerusalem, and for the entire world. He was aware that what he saw in the city looked devastatingly different from those moments in the garden—before the bad and the ugly entered the human story. Certainly, he experienced the heartbreaking tension of watching what he had created, with such care and attention, fall into the wrong hands. Yet he saw glimmers of what used to be beautiful and glorious, and what, because of the saving work he would do, would soon be beautiful again.

Jesus was very familiar with the good, bad, and ugly of our world. But instead of responding with contempt, he showed incredible, never-before-seen, and hard-to-understand love. The author of Hebrews—a letter written to Christians in the first century—describes this love: "[Keep] our eyes on Jesus, the source and perfecter of our faith. For the joy that lay before him, he endured the cross, despising the shame, and sat down at the right hand of the throne of God" (12:2).

Jesus saw something we don't often see, and I wonder if we miss seeing it for ourselves because we don't often sacrificially love with joy as Jesus does. What was "set before" Jesus that produced so much joy, in spite of the reality that he was being crucified and shamed by, quite frankly, all of us?

The letter of Revelation describes the city that God is preparing for eternity. In this letter, we find a description of what I believe Jesus saw as he hung on the cross: "There will no longer be any curse. The throne of God and of the Lamb [Jesus] will be in the city, and his servants will worship him" (22:3).

Jesus was fascinated not with a city driven by an impulsive, selfish ambition, but with a city driven by the beauty and undeserved grace of the cross that he himself bore. Jesus was and is fascinated by a city made up of those who esteem him, his sacrifice, and the fruits of that life more than anything else. Although Jesus was profoundly affected by the brokenness of the city of Jerusalem, he was much more fascinated with the city that would be ushered in by his selfless and sacrificial love. His familiarity with the brokenness of Jerusalem strengthened him to draw near in love rather than to push away in contempt. That vision of a city was the joy set before him.

Consider a couple who has been married for a long time. Why are we so surprised by marriages that last longer than ten years? And we're even more surprised when we hear why they have stayed together as long as they have. Some say, "Growing deeper in our relationship and learning about my spouse has been the most compelling journey." Really? Thirty-five years together isn't enough time to learn everything you need to know about a person?

Their response seems simplistic, but beneath that response often seems to be fascination and hope. That response is saying, "I know we've been together for a long time, but with every passing moment the very nature of love has persuaded me to stay through the dark times as well as through the exciting times. I know that time will always offer us new ways to contribute to who we're both being shaped to be."

All thriving relationships have this woven into their fabric—not just marriages. I'm talking about hope, fascination, and interest. As my good friend Kenny always says, "I'd rather be interested than interesting." God is at work in people and places, and he's involved because he cares. God is deeply interested in our lives. He says through one of his prophets, "As I live . . . I take no pleasure in the death of the wicked, but rather that the wicked person should turn from his way and live. Repent, repent of your evil ways! Why will you die, house of Israel?" (Ezek. 33:11). Although this word is direct and hard, it is fueled by deep interest, fascination, and hope. God offers us the honor of being part of that process for others through relationship. We have the privilege of joining him in the renewal of cities and cultures.

It's been seven years since I moved back to the same neighborhood where I lived for more than two decades. We had been living upstate in Rochester, New York, about a six-hour drive from a good cup of authentic *avena* with a Dominican touch—which is mostly found in Washington Heights. There's no question—I am biased about which New York City neighborhood is the best. But to be honest, when we started making arrangements to move back, and even after settling in the first few months, I felt some tension. I was excited, but I was also afraid. What would Uptown look like after six years? How would the city receive me, now that I had a family? Would I be able to afford it? What would the neighborhood think of my ambitions for it? So much of the city and community was changing, and I wondered if I would love it the same way I had years ago. Could I even love it the same anymore?

I came in with so many questions, and even some doubts. I was afraid that the community, the city, and the people had changed so much that I wouldn't be able to love it the same or love it well. I was afraid that what I was feeling was nostalgia rather than ambition or compassion. I was afraid that what I was really longing for was the Uptown of my childhood while making no room for the Uptown that could be. Then I suddenly realized that I had changed as much as the city had. I realized that change is inevitable in our experience, and the city was a part of that. The goal is to change well, to grow in love. The journey, in large part, is about learning to experience a radical, dynamic, yet uncompromising love that accepts you as you are but could never leave you as you are. I realized that we needed to familiarize ourselves with the story of this place again—its past and present—in order to shape its future. We needed to tell the story the only way we could: through our experiences. Although it is true that this place has been my home for as long as I can remember, every day I'm learning to love it again.

New York city is the largest and least loved city in America. Why would it be loved. It is never the same city in a dozen years. If a man finds a few houses from his past not yet leveled, he is fortunate.

—Harper Herald, 1924

CHAPTER 1

Plant Roots: 'Tate Quieto!

Have you ever been in a sea of people and realized that, although they're in the city you call home, they're still just nameless faces? Of course you have. Perhaps you haven't if you're from a small country town, but most of our global cities have millions of people in them. It's absurd to think that you can know everyone.

If your family is anything like mine, the feeling is similar to being at one of those outrageous family parties. There isn't a soul sitting down. (Well, perhaps *abuelo* is. He can go days without getting off his recliner.) Everyone is on the dance floor, which is really just your living room floor after half your furniture gets pushed to one side of the room. Quite honestly, the floor shakes like there's a herd of wild animals running

21

on it. Kids are screaming and running around playing "red light, green light" while the adults dance *un perico ripiao encendio*, as my uncle Bonilla would say. Every member of the family is there, from second cousins to uncles younger than you to *primo-hermanos* (not your typical relative, just a super-close friend of the family). They're all there, and with every new person you greet, it gets more outrageous—but also, somehow, more refreshingly memorable. The time offers you a microscopic sense of familiarity and closeness, but the sense of distance is still there—only because, like I said earlier, you just don't know everybody intimately. You say to yourself, *I know you're my family and I'm supposed to know you, but I kind of don't.*

This is my face when I'm expected to know everyone at the party.

The city can make you feel this way. The easy thing to do is to walk into the train, look around, find that corner seat that you were hoping would be vacant, pop your Beats in, and listen to your playlist while you disconnect from everyone. I've done it on a number of occasions. But then the feeling changes a bit when you jump off the train and head back into your neighborhood. You know the people here. You give somebody a head nod, or show some love with a *"qué lo que!"* There is a sense of comfort here because you're home. These are the folks you see at the bodega, the barbershop, the ball courts, or the playgrounds where you take your kids to see what dirt really tastes like. You know this place.

Now, it would be ridiculous for me to say that you know all of these people intimately, but there is a sense of closeness. You deal with the same train delays. You get the same neighbor discount from the coffee shop. You have *la doña* (sweet, grandmother-kind-of neighbor) watch your kids play outside from her ground-floor window while you run an errand or finish dinner. For me, there's something just slightly different in this environment. There is a sense of family here. The Hispanics here had no one else with whom to build that sense of family, so they did it with each other. They immigrated to this neighborhood in Manhattan and never moved away. Whether because of fear, miseducation, or familiarity, they stayed put—and in the process, although perhaps unintentionally, they created this sense of rootedness, this feeling of home.

As Simple as the Color Yellow

On a recent trip to Argentina, I sat next to a gentleman named Rodrigo, who was traveling from his hometown of Trelew to Buenos Aires on business. We engaged in small talk for a bit, but then I became really intrigued when he began to talk about the color yellow. Yes, the color. Rodrigo said yellow was the color of the walls of a coffee shop near his home. He was strangely specific about it, but I enjoyed that. He said that yellow reminded him of the flowers at his grandmother's house where he was raised, just a couple of blocks from that same coffee shop. Poetic, right? Rodrigo appreciated the nostalgia triggered by the yellow walls so much that he visited that coffee shop often, making it part of his regular morning routine. He made great friends there and even met his wife in that coffee shop. Amazing! He said that no matter where he traveled and what beauty he saw as he traveled, his love for the people and colors of his city would always draw him back. Can you imagine the kind of love he felt for his city? Granted, we were on the plane for about three hours and the conversation didn't start until about an hour into the flight. If we had talked longer, I would have learned about his fears, concerns, and gripes concerning his city. But the first things he talked about were his experiences and memories of being planted in his city. The colors, smells, and people had such a profound place in his heart that they would always draw him back.

As I listened to Rodrigo, I asked myself a few questions. What kind of imprint could I leave on the world if I paid this much attention to my own city and my community? How deeply and loudly would my life speak into the lives of those around me—my wife, kids, neighbors, and those under my leadership—if I took this kind of interest in them and the community? Would I leverage my influence to grow meaningful relationships that lead people to the ultimate experience of love and meaning that's found in Jesus?

Over the last few years, I have realized that loving our cities well demands that we know our cities well. It seems natural, right? What aspects of our cities should we be celebrating because they reflect what God has envisioned? What are the idols of my city—those things or people that overpromise and underdeliver? In what ways can the city grow? Where and how has God called the church to play a role?

I realized that if I was going to contribute to the much-needed reform in culture, personally and as a spiritual leader in my community, I was going to have to plant roots here—a tall order, for sure, and intimidating in some ways. But why does this matter? Because I'm convinced more than ever that in our constantly changing culture, anything that takes root will take time. And if we, as kingdom-of-God citizens, don't look to the long haul, we won't have a considerable effect. Time will be one of our greatest assets. Risk will be one of our closest friends. Transforming love will be our greatest motivation. Is it worth our time? Is it worth the risk? Is it worth the sacrifice? Ask any kid who doesn't have a dad or big brother. Ask the parents working long hours to make sure their kids have book bags for school. Ask the young girl who sees no other way to feel accepted and cared for than to give herself away to men. Ask the older gentleman who feels enslaved by his ambition to climb the financial ladder. Ask the immigrants who quietly move about the community, gripped by fear because they're unable to communicate in a foreign country. Ask them. They will all say that it is worth the time, risk, and sacrifice.

Doing More with What You Know

We have some great neighbors—some we know casually, others we know a little better, and others we know as friends. José and Lilly, our neighbors from upstairs, are our friends. My wife has built an intimate friendship with Lilly; they're both young mothers living in the craziness of New York City. Lilly is a schoolteacher and José works on the New York University campus. Anna and I realized how difficult it was for them, during the school year, to manage their schedules and find babysitting for their little boy, Nathan. Because of their conflicting schedules, they reached a point where they swapped baby duty at the 116th train station, as Lilly was on her way home and José was going in to work, even in the bitter cold. They didn't seem to think much of it. It was tough, I'm sure, but they probably thought to themselves, *Hey, this is what it is and we have to get it done.*

But Anna and I saw friends who worked hard, and parents who would go to great lengths in caring for their son. We saw that God had blessed us with significantly flexible work schedules. And ultimately, all those variables added up to an opportunity to help our friends. So we did. We loved them in the way that seemed most practical. We can't quite remember how it all started, but with our flexible schedules, Anna and I made ourselves available to watch Nathan while Lilly made it home from work. On some occasions, we encouraged Lilly to take a couple of minutes to detox from her day before picking up Nathan at our apartment. Even when she came to pick Nathan up, she would often stay at our apartment for some hangout time.

We deeply value those times, because they provide a fresh picture of how a Christian family engages its neighbors and community. I don't share this experience to showcase what great neighbors we are, not in the least. I share this story so that you can capture the principle that a healthy perception of your community demands genuine and intentional engagement with it. In other words, you cannot sit on the sidelines if you're trying to know and love those in your community.

Walking the City

Let's go to Acts 17 for a moment. Although it easily can go unnoticed, Luke uses a couple of key words to describe what Paul does when he settles in Athens, Greece. In verse 22, Paul makes a confident assertion about the Athenians. He says, "I see that you are extremely religious in every respect." What follows is the *major key* (as DJ Khaled would say), so watch closely. The word *for* is used. This is important, because it will tell us why Paul is so confident in his assertion about them. Luke goes on to say in verse 23, "For as I was passing through and observing the objects of your worship, I even found an altar on which was inscribed: 'To an Unknown God.'" Why should these words be blowing your mind? Because they are the most practically helpful words any Christian in any city looking to share Jesus with anyone can hear. Paul *passed through, observed,* and *found* things in the city of Athens. His perception that they were religious people didn't come from mere intuition or a stereotype. And quite frankly, it didn't come from a special revelation from God. It came simply from Paul walking the city and taking the time to know it.

Paul goes on to share some memorable words about faith with a very non-Christian crowd. But what makes this all the more profound and effective are the words that follow his long spiel to the Athenians about this *unknown god* they serve. "When they heard . . . some people joined him and believed" (Acts 17:32, 34). Paul's words proved to be timely for the Athenians. Paul understood the Athenian context; he traveled around the city to learn what was good and bad about Athens, and who their idols were. And with his burning passion to make God known, Paul shared some timely words. It resulted in some people mocking him, other people wanting to continue the conversation, and finally a group of people who needed no more convincing that the God of the Bible was the true God.

The perception we have of our cities and communities determines our service toward them. If we see people only from our fire escapes, and not from street level, we handicap our ability to serve. We miss the details. We miss those things that are important to people in our neighborhoods. It should be important to us who the *bodegero* is, who our neighbors are, who our kids' teachers are, what our coworkers go home to, and why that elderly lady with a bad leg walks around the neighborhood with a worried look on her face. Those things should interest us because, like Paul, we want our personal engagements to be timely, thoughtful, and life giving. If we forgo intimacy with our communities, we relinquish any opportunity for meaningful service and transformation. Knowing our communities will give us a bull's-eye target—the idols that need to be destroyed, the weaknesses that need to be served, and the strengths that need to be celebrated.

Rosanne Cash, daughter of the late Johnny Cash, once said this about New York: "I had rules for myself about my New Yorker-ness. I had to show the city I respected it and that I cared enough to learn about it."[1] In the end, you can come to know New York—or any city, for that matter—only when you commit yourself to her. Commit to hearing her dreams, her values, and her fears. Commit to her growth. Commit to fighting things that bring harm to her. Commit to sitting and listening to her story.

The Investment Monster

All of this commitment can be summed up in one word—*investment*. Investing is no easy task, perhaps because of the nature of the word itself. Investment is a finance term, and we don't always like talking about money, especially when the conversation has to do with giving money up. People are private about many things, but about nothing more than money—our bank account, credit, and stocks. I'm not suggesting that we walk around shouting our credit scores, or even that we should share them with other people. I am saying that it's difficult to talk about money because we so closely identify with how much of it we do or don't have.

Here's a simple definition of investment: putting personal resources into something that offers potential future return. No matter how you flip it, investing involves risk. We give up personal resources now so that they will—in time—flourish and yield greater fruit. More than often, that proves to be difficult because it demands a hopeful vision of the future, and sometimes our present realities cloud that vision for us.

Perhaps this story will help. In 2003, my older sister and my brother-in-law persuaded my parents to invest in life insurance. My dad was your typical blue-collar working immigrant from the Dominican Republic, and my mom had finally settled at home after working for several years as a teacher's aide and home attendant. My parents were able to lock in a quote where my dad paid $90.00 a month. If anything happened to either of them, my family would receive $100,000—no questions asked. After about a year, my dad found it difficult to keep up with the payments because of all his other expenses, so he decided to cut it off. No more life insurance. In 2005, my mother received a diagnosis of cancer. In 2007, she passed away. This was no small episode in my life. In fact, it was one of the most powerful and life-altering moments of my life, but I'll leave those details for later. Needless to say, her death was devastating, and also created a huge financial burden that loomed over us. The idea of life insurance or savings—for my family and, quite frankly, for most immigrant families—was a luxury. It wasn't a pressing reality because what was pressing was the immediate present—rent, food, lights—but not death, although we knew it would come eventually. We didn't plan for the future, although we knew we should.

Now let me be clear about this. My dad was emotionally, mentally, and physically involved in my life, as he still is today. He is a great man, and I thank God for his example. But with all great people, we can also learn from their lapses in judgment or their shortcomings. And just like my dad, most of us fail to invest in a vision that goes beyond *right now*. As an immigrant with no college degree—just the grit in his hands—my dad was working to give us a place to live, food to eat, clothes to wear, and an education to help us excel. The thought of life insurance or savings was too foreign for him, despite the brevity and frailty of life. He pushed it to the back of his mind and ignored it, because of the reality of immigrant life in America—and particularly in New York. There's often not much you can do, even though you know that it's sensible to think about your family's financial future. Because of personal disinvestment, a lack of equal opportunity, and/or the immense pressure that the lack of opportunity creates, your only option becomes to cut even the *lean meat*. In other words, my father's circumstances trapped him into making a decision that he would regret later—and he did. For a while, it haunted him. His inability to see beyond the *now* had kept him from investing $90.00 a month, which would have resulted in $100,000 for our family during an unexpected and turbulent season later. In his case, investment was scared away by the monster called *the present*.

Faithful investment in the city *now* happens as a result of a faithful and hopeful vision of the city's *future*. How we see our cities determines how we invest in them. At the heart of investment is what Casey Gerald of MBAs Across America says: "I'll take the risk and I'll take the lead because I'm betting on the future."[2] The future can be nebulous and hard to see, but our confidence is in the one who holds the future— God. If we see the city the same way most New Yorkers see Grand Central Station—as a gateway to where we really want to go, or as a place that we marvel at but never really settle into—then our investment will most likely be superficial and insignificant. In fact, it will make us consumers of the city, rather than contributors to the city. We will find no motivation to significantly give for our city's benefit. But we can challenge ourselves to see our cities in the way that God sees them, and we can remind ourselves that although we don't see as many stars and breathtaking natural landscapes as people in other places do, there are more images of God here in the city than in any other place in the world. Although mountain ranges, valleys, and the deep oceans have been drawn by the finger of God, it is people—you and me—who are actually created in his image. There are just under two million of us on the island of Manhattan alone. God is restoring all things through Jesus, and he's beginning with people.

If we truly grasped and believed this idea, I wonder how that would shift the way we invest. Considering that trust takes time, influence grows from relationships, and anything significant very seldom happens overnight—I wonder how much more willing we would be to plant ourselves in our cities.

Learning to Take Risks

Anyone who knows me knows that my wife and kids are precious to me. I see them as gifts from God for me to enjoy, and I grow through my relationship with them. They're also precious to me because I see my family—my kids particularly—as opportunities for legacy building. I love my city and my neighborhood, and I'm planted here. But I'm also realistic. I know that I won't be around forever, but I pray that my kids will be around after me. What will I be proud to see them herald? What banner do I hope to see them wave? What life message will the city that I love so much hear from my kids?

I have two great kids, both born in New York. But it seems to me that having a significant influence on the city, based on my vision of hope and restoration, calls for the investment of some of my most precious things—namely, the people I love. In trying to love my city as Jesus does, I've been challenged to say not only that I had kids in the city, but also that I raised kids in the city—not as a boast, but as a means to love. I am willing to raise my kids here, although many people would find it nearly impossible to do so.

When we raise our children to be adults, we leave our cities with men and women who love them, invest in them, and have a hopeful and healthy vision for them. We hope that our children will do the same with their children, and that in the generations to come, our cities will have an army of God-fearing, faithful, loving, and committed citizens.

My wife and I wrestled with this idea when our son was transitioning from kindergarten to first grade. From three years old, my son had been enrolled in a private Christian school. It was a phenomenal experience. He made many friends and has many great memories. But we felt he was losing touch with the world outside of his experience. He's a pastor's kid who spends most of his time around our friends from church, and he was attending a private Christian school. I don't say this to make it seem like a bad thing, but I could understand why he was blown away at the thought of someone not loving God the way we do, if at all.

So my wife and I did our homework. We researched public schools in our district and found the one with which we were most happy. It was a great school—great teacher-student ratio, great staff, and an active parent association. We were happy, but we were also nervous. It was going to be the first time, in his school setting, that Jo was not going to be part of the majority. It was going to be the first time that the teachers didn't open the school day with a prayer. It was going to be the first time that Jo would not be able to freely mention God without facing some kind of consequence, big or small. We feared that he could get into trouble with his teachers or be ridiculed by his classmates, but we moved forward. Why? For a couple of reasons. First, we were comforted by the kind of home in which he was being raised. We knew the God whom we as a family serve, and we knew the spiritual climate from which Jo was coming. Second, and this was probably the main reason, we wanted our son to learn to love his neighbor. *Neighbor* can be a misleading word, because we often limit its definition to the people around us geographically. But *neighbor* encompasses more than that. Neighbors can be next door, they can be on your team, or they can be on the other team. You have your family, and then everyone else is your neighbor. Yes, everyone else.

At times, Jo was so surprised by people who didn't share our beliefs and love for Jesus that he almost didn't know what to do with them. Sometimes he would disengage altogether. But if we wanted him to grow in his love for his neighbor, he needed to be around them. We also wanted him to learn that we can sometimes serve as mirrors to one another. If Jo saw disregard for God in one of his nonbelieving classmates, for example, he might realize that same disregard exists in himself in some way.

Our decision to transition our son from a private Christian school to a public school was an investment. We prayed, sought counsel, and "planted" our son in the soil of our community, so that one day, God would raise him up to love this community as deeply as God himself does. Our decision wasn't prescriptive. We're not inviting every family reading this to pull their kids from private Christian schools. Our decision was thoughtful, prayerful, and intentional, and it was the right one for us. We saw an opportunity to be more involved in our son's life and to help shape his perception of the world—and we took it. This was an opportunity to be our son's "first responder" when crisis hits, and when things aren't neatly packaged in a Christian worldview. Before he could learn it anywhere else, we wanted him to learn it from us. But our decision also represented a long-term investment in society, and in our city in particular. If we can help our son have a healthy view of God and other people, and as a result develop a deep sense of love and obligation to his world, we will be investing into our city a young man willing to serve the city.

If you're not convinced by my story, consider God's investment. In a far more powerful way than I did, he planted his Son, Jesus, in the soil of this world with the plan to raise many more with him. God looked at our broken world and dreamed for it a vision that far exceeds what it is today. God's story reminds us that "when the time came to completion, God sent his Son, born of a woman, born under the law [under the limitations of a broken humanity], to redeem those under the law, so that we might receive adoption as sons" (Gal. 4:4–5). After sending his Son, God allowed Jesus to suffer and be planted in the ground, but only so that he might rise to life, like a seed rises to be a plant. God knew that the investment of his Son into the world would produce faith, hope, and ultimately, our renewal. The beauty and goodness of heaven is being made real here, in our world, in our cities, through God's church. This is why we hear Jesus challenging us to "pray like this: Our Father in heaven. . . . Your kingdom come. Your will be done on earth as it is in heaven" (Matt. 6:9–11).

What does investment look like for you?

Share the Story, Build the Culture

Change is nothing new to our city, nor is it new for my community. For people who can't hang with some of the changes, it can feel like the bully in elementary school who constantly shoved you, poked fun at you, and tried to embarrass you in front of everyone in the cafeteria. For me, planting myself in this city over the last eight years has meant learning what it means to preserve what's here now while also making room for the new cultures moving in. Uptown hasn't always been a predominantly Hispanic community, but for the last four and a half decades the major culture here has been Dominican. The two major experiences for me growing up were bodegas and restaurants with an endless array of *moro de guandules, arroz blanco, pollo a la brasa, aguacate, tostones y costillitas.* Today those bodegas and restaurants risk becoming extinct.

As a kid, everything about a trip to the bodega was an adventure for me, and that hasn't changed much now that I'm an adult. Bodegas are an oasis from the craziness of the world around us. Simply put, a bodega is a corner store. But as Fernando Mateo said, they're also "a place where people get together and go over their daily news and become part of their communities."[3] When I was a kid, being sent to the bodega was probably one of the most exciting things I could do on a school day. Kids in my neighborhood didn't have Boy Scouts, and we didn't have retreats to look forward to during our school breaks. Instead, we looked forward to being sent to the bodega, which wasn't just a simple trip to the corner store. We knew it, and our parents knew it—no matter how urgently my mom needed that carton of milk from the store. Even our friends downstairs playing *vitilla* knew it. (Greatest game ever! Go look it up.) A trip to the bodega really meant a half game of *vitilla*, five minutes of twenty-one (a free-for-all basketball game with a bunch of kids from the block), two Hail Mary throws in the middle of the street, and, of course, two attempts at roofing those classic one-dollar, blue, Sky Bounce balls. Bodegas were a place where, as an American-born Dominican, I would be reminded of my culture. *Merengue* played from a pair of dusty, beat-up speakers hanging off the shelf that held the yellow dishwashing gloves. A handful of men sat on milk crates outside the store, politickin' about *el PRD y el PLD*, two political parties in the Dominican government. But more than anything, bodegas felt like home base. You could go to a bodega and they knew you. They knew your parents and, more often than not, they knew what you had been sent to buy. Your mom had called the store to make sure you got there and picked up the right thing. (Or maybe that was just my mom?) But here's the thing. Even with the cramped aisles, the fat cat who sat by the *plátanos* barely opening his eyes, and the loud politickin', bodegas offered what we needed—yes, the items for which our mothers had sent us, but more important, a sense of belonging and affirmation.

In 2015, seventy-five bodegas were closed down in neighborhoods that had been historically Hispanic, including Inwood and Washington Heights.[4] This may seem natural for some readers, but if bodegas go, we lose a rich part of what this neighborhood has been for many decades. This might be the natural progression of neighborhoods, but that's precisely what I believe we need to push against—by sticking around and planting our roots. I've always wondered what the answer could be to Usnavi's question at the end of *In the Heights*, the Broadway play that brought great pride to our neighborhood: "In five years when this city is all rich folks and hipsters, who's gonna miss this raggedy little business?"[5] (Usnavi is referring to his bodega on 181st.) We will. We will miss the raggedy little business. Bodegas aren't just simple corner stores where we go in and pick up what we need. No, bodegas help our parents' generation feel comfortable and accepted here, as they transition into a foreign land. Bodegas help us, the second generation, whose future is here, to build empathy for people on the margins—the foreigner, the stranger trying to make a home and leave a legacy for his children, the people who deeply know what the margins feel like. Bodegas help preserve our heritage and grow a healthy sense of ethnic pride—a valuable commodity for minorities. They help people who are trying to retain their heritage in an often-uninviting foreign land.

This bodega was the destination of many of my adventures as a kid growing up in Uptown.

Losing bodegas isn't the real tragedy. Losing compassion for other people, and empathy for those who are hurting, and justice for all—that's the real tragedy. Early in my Christian journey, my faith was simple and practical. It was about how much life reflects what I believed about Jesus and his sacrifice for me. Somewhere in the journey, it became mainly about learning propositions and formulating arguments about my Christian faith. I don't mean to peg the practicality of Christianity against learning and the intellectual aspects of Christianity. James tells us that one is the fruit of the other (see James 2:14–24). The two collaborate in the Christian's life. But God's desire is to see neighborhoods actually transformed by his truth, his take on love, his take on mercy and forgiveness, his take on unity. The journey to see renewed or—as some people prefer to call them—enriched neighborhoods isn't an economic plan that defines better communities as richer communities. The journey to building the communities we wish to see is found in a constant, faithful, personal, powerful God who doesn't change, even when change is as common as a cold in our lives.

Although I value progress, I also value constants. We've become very familiar with transiency, but I think we could use some things in our lives that don't change. The journey to building the communities we wish to see is found in the transformation of the people who make them. We need news that can remind people on both sides of Broadway—in all socioeconomic classes—that accumulating wealth and status doesn't satisfy us, nor does it position us to grow to be better any more than the next thing we set our hearts on. The beauty about Jesus is that his news is for everyone, whether you have a lot or little. It's like Paul tells us in Philippians 4:12–13: "I know both how to make do with a little, and I know how to make do with a lot. In any and all circumstances I have learned the secret of being content—whether well fed or hungry, whether in abundance or in need. I am able to do all things through him who strengthens me."

Why does this matter deeply to me? And why should it matter deeply to anyone who shares the human experience, especially people who consider themselves Christians? Well, to put it simply, God cares, and so should we. The story of God rallies around a simple truth. People lacked not only words with which to communicate, but also—and perhaps even more crippling—the wherewithal to know that things weren't as they should be. Yet God in his infinite wisdom gave us words—or better yet, gave us his living Word to restore what had been lost.

When I look at my neighborhood and see families losing their apartments and businesses, I can't help but ask how the richness of a culture isn't worth more than the profit from a new luxury apartment complex going up. Many families have been fighting to stick around. Many families have fought to help preserve the stories in the neighborhood, but many unfortunately have lost faith, energy, and hope. I hope that telling their stories and sharing in their struggle helps to preserve the culture. I hope that it helps build the culture in ways so that every demographic and both sides of Broadway can benefit. I hope that telling the stories of people who often don't have the voice or the platform to do so themselves will help rekindle their hope, faith, and efforts.

I know that encouraging one family to see the value of planting roots won't change the landscape of the city. However, just one family fighting to be heard could start the divine revolution of God transforming our neighborhoods and cities through his people.

> For the needy will not always be forgotten; the hope of the oppressed will not perish forever.
> —Psalm 9:18

Dear Lennie

There is another, perhaps equally important side to encouraging people to plant roots. Maybe John Steinbeck's classic novella, *Of Mice and Men,* can help us understand. The novella is the story of two migrant workers in California chasing their dream of one day buying their own plot of land. George was the uneducated but incredibly savvy one. Lennie, he was quite different. He was large in stature, had mental disabilities, and an insatiable desire to pet soft things—rabbits, in particular. Their journey led them through a series of interesting turns, challenges, and in the end, a heart-wrenching tragedy.

Lennie's incomparable size and blaring unawareness proved to be a recipe for disaster. His desire to coddle things resulted in many of them dying in the hands of his brute and blind strength. In every scenario Lennie was well-intended, yet the outcome was always the same—his presence was fatally overpowering.

I was once asked by a good friend, "Rich, what does it look like for a guy like me [white guy] to plant myself in a predominantly minority community in healthy ways?" After thinking carefully about the delicate nature of the question, I responded with, "Have you

read *Of Mice and Men*? Let me tell you about Lennie."
I went on to describe Lennie's character and some of
the parallels to the answer he was looking for. Let me
be clear—in the book, Lennie's character is disabled,
but that is not what I am highlighting here, nor am I
saying that those from the dominant culture are disabled. Rather, what I was hoping to communicate to
my buddy has a general unawareness that both share.

I've seen Uptown change over the years—you've
already heard me share about Uptown losing many of
its bodegas, a staple to the Hispanic experience. And
the truth is that we could argue that there are several
reasons for the change. Disinvestment from the locals,
urban planning, the natural progression of cities. But
in large part, many of our neighborhoods with a large
population of minorities have seen significant changes
because their stories aren't considered, and as a result,
they're not valued. Unfortunately, in comparison to
other narratives in our city, their story just isn't told
enough, celebrated enough, or preserved enough. Our
burden is that the Hispanic experience is on the brink
of extinction and only a few are concerned.

As my buddy and I wrestled through his question,
I continued on to note that as many well-intended
dominant-culture people move into these communities,

there's a sense in which they exist more as residents than they do as neighbors. Growing up there were few people in the community that you knew nothing about, or that weren't involved in your life in some way. Whether it was *la china* from the cleaners, who knew you were supposed to pick up your dad's work uniform, or *abuelita* on the fifth floor who babysat you while your mom was out running errands, people knew you. There was a sense that neighbors were very different from residents. Neighbors *make* the neighborhood; residents *exist* in the neighborhood. Residents come and go. They're in and out. And there's little involvement with or investment in the stories of others, particularly with those who don't look like them. On the other hand, neighbors carry a sense of responsibility to one another. They're involved in each other's stories in some form. There is a sense in which their neighbors' good is their good.

This is far from what my experience as a Dominican-American has been with a gentrifying Uptown. I've spent most of this chapter sharing my experiences and faith with the hopes to inspire a more rooted culture among us, especially those of faith. But I'd be foolish to propose that rootedness looks the same for all people groups.

I have the honor to lead a great church community with amazing people. As I lead this group of diverse people in our young and growing church, I've observed some postures that have been helpful to those from the dominant culture as they look to plant roots in our predominantly minority communities.

Humility, Not Pride

The blindness that we often see in those of the dominant culture has communicated more pride than humility. But I'll confess, humility innately carries a difficult task for most in our culture: "Consider others as more important than yourselves. Everyone should look out not only for his own interests, but also for the interests of others" (Phil. 2:3–4). This is as much a charge for the locals in the community as it is for those transplanting themselves into the community. But in a place where the minority narrative isn't celebrated or valued as much as others, it's significantly helpful when the dominant culture is aware of their size and power and uses them not only for their good, but more important, for the good of locals who exist there—the less privileged and powerless. If a posture of humility is absent, the minority narrative is looked at with contempt, forgotten, and ultimately replaced.

After several tough conversations with my buddy on the topic, he came to realize that humility for him as a white guy in a predominately Hispanic community could only mean one thing: a neighbor that comes under the leadership of a minority. It was obvious that coming to this conclusion was deeply confronting him. But he was convinced that it was the only way to exist if he wanted to be a neighbor and not merely a resident. He realized he couldn't just cozy up in an apartment west of Broadway (historically, the more affluent side of our neighborhood) just because he could. He realized he couldn't just flippantly advocate for new luxury developments in the community just because he liked the culture it would bring to the neighborhood. He realized that always shopping at big chains like Starbucks was slowly (in some cases, faster than others) pushing mom-and-pop shops out of the community that have been there for decades. He realized that without this sort of humility it would make it difficult to connect, deepen, and thrive in relationship. He realized that only this sort of humility would allow him to be a neighbor and not a resident.

Yet in no way am I saying that you *must* make these lifestyle adjustments. The only way to foster authentic decisions like these is to inspire someone's will, not manipulate it. Humility is a posture that demands intentionality and sacrifice; it demands a compelling example. It's sacrifice and not entitlement that inspires authentic relationship. In the end, thriving communities are not monolithic communities, where one group or culture runs the show. Instead, the kind of humility I'm referring to is revolutionary—quite literally helping to shift the way neighborhoods exist. Humility inspires people to live differently toward one another and, more important, honors the stories that have existed before your own by dignifying them rather disregarding them.

Partnership, Not Paternalism

I've always admired my *viejo*. For close to thirty years he worked in this country, without much complaining. As a kid I was grateful that my dad worked enough and earned enough that he would buy me *y mi hermana* the latest Jordans every once in a while. He provided both physically and emotionally. *Siempre hubo comida*, we vacationed in the summer (even if it was just to my aunt's house in Atlantic City), and he put us through school. We had what we needed and very few times, if ever, did he need anything from us.

Yet over the years, it's been interesting to see our relationship slowly evolve. Certainly, my pops is still an important person in my life, but practically and perhaps even emotionally, I don't need him as much. In fact, as I spend more and more time with him now that he's retired, I realize he needs me just as much as I needed him back when I was a teenager. He remarried after my mother's death and he's got children around the age of my own children. He's got some health issues and is constantly asking me to join him in the gym to make sure he's staying in shape. And we're not just exercising in the gym. Those visits to the gym are usually accompanied with the occasional conversation about God, marriage, and parenting. Those moments show me that *el viejo* needs me too. Not because he's incapable or because he's emotionally unstable, but because over the years, we've both realized that we need each other in different ways.

This is what may be missing from some of our gentrifying communities: a sense of interdependence. It seems as though most of our white friends move in with an intention to give help, but not receive help. To offer change, but not receive change for themselves. To teach and train and rebuild, but not learn and grow themselves. To pursue revitalization, but not to discover the life that lies in the very areas they're looking to change. While it is true that inner-city neighborhoods are plagued with fatherlessness, as my friend and pastor Kenny would say, "Inner-city neighborhoods don't need a hand up or a hand down, we need a hand across." Inner-city neighborhoods don't need the dominant culture to act as our father, we need them to act as our friends. We need partnership, not paternalism.

Not only does this put us on trajectory toward thriving as a community, but it's faithful to God's desire for us. From the very beginning it was God's desire for the human experience to be an experience of interdependence. Consider Genesis 1. In the Bible, God goes into great detail describing how all things came to be. But what strikes me as most interesting about this account is the tension between sameness and difference. In the Genesis 1 story, we see heaven and earth; land and sea; day and night; light and dark; Creator and creation; and of course, we see male and female. We are created from and in the image of God, which communicates the sameness of our make up and experience. Yet there is also a sense in which we are different and unique in design. There is a sense in which, while we are different, we still need each other.

In a conversation about race relations, my homie and pastor Abe Cho comments on the mystery of the Genesis 1 account. He says, "God himself—the mystery of who God is, in the biblical faith—is a God who himself [embodies] interdependent difference. If you want to understand how God's creation works, interdependence and difference is at the heart of [the conversation]."[6] Genesis 2:18 is perhaps where it becomes most convincing for me. This Scripture isn't simply a verse to be quoted at weddings or marriage conferences, but this is a verse that describes all of human relationship. God says, "It is not good for the man to be alone. I will make a helper corresponding to him." While it is true that in a sense this verse shows us the interdependent nature of the marriage relationship, it also shows that for any of us, existing in isolation was never God's intention. Perhaps even more significant, this passage of Scripture shows us that only together—women, men, young, old, black, brown, white, affluent, marginalized, blue-collar, white-collar, rich, poor, gentrified, gentrifier, east of Broadway, west of Broadway—under the banner of God's purposes, can we display the fullness of who God is. The moment we believe that we are the only ones that can make meaningful contributions is the moment we see ourselves as more valuable, the moment we strip the image of God from those around us. In other words, your contribution is better because it's coming from a source (you) that doesn't need help or support or improvement, at least not more that those receiving your help. Self-value is tied to assets, resources, and circumstance. We have conditioned ourselves to think that needing help or needing to be served makes one less than. That is perhaps why we are so eager to help, but not so eager to receive it.

God created the entire universe to exist in interdependent difference. Only under the banner of a God who cares deeply enough to not obliterate our differences, but to leverage them for his redemptive purposes, can we truly discover who we are and what our purpose is. Martin Luther King Jr. said it this way: "In a real sense all life is inter-related. All men are caught in an inescapable network of mutuality, tied in a single garment of destiny. Whatever affects one directly, affects all indirectly. I can never be what I ought to be until you are what you ought to be, and you can never be what you ought to be until I am what I ought to be. This is the inter-related structure of reality."[7]

If we don't encourage these postures, what is at stake?

The Beautiful Difference

For one, we silence the beautiful difference of the minority story. Without a posture of humility and partnership we perpetuate a narrative that promotes white dominance. I know that sounds brash, but here's what I mean: It's a narrative that says that while it is true that all cultures are important, white culture is most important. It's a narrative that says that while it's true that all cultures have something to contribute, white culture's contribution is most meaningful. If we don't strongly encourage this posture of partnership instead of paternalism, our experiences with Christianity can also become dangerously oppressive with this thinking. If we're seen as a charity instead of as partners, it becomes increasingly difficult for minorities to believe that we have intrinsic worth and value as image bearers of God. The goal becomes to be saved by Jesus, *and* to look like the white person who shared the news of Jesus. There is a greater chance that we spiral down in self-hatred than flourish in godly confidence, courage, and leadership. In a talk on Latin American Theology, Juan Martinez exposes the heart of paternalism. He says, "The perception is that Latinos can only be the object of mission and not missionaries themselves."[8] In this deficient frame of thinking, salvation does not belong to the Lord—as Jonah and the Psalms would remind us (Jonah 2:9; Ps. 3:8)—but salvation belongs to the dominant culture.

Second, we miss the opportunity for optimum growth. If we were designed to need each other, then life seems off, curtailed, and in some ways, short-circuited, if we are not in the rhythm of having a variety of voices in our lives.

The good news of Jesus is far too challenging to disregard our need for one another. The beauty is that, in his death, our tendency to segregate ourselves can also be put to death. In his resurrection we discover the power and courage to confront the dark past and, only after, live unified in our differences in order to display the goodness and peace of God in our cities—a far more compelling and inspiring picture of God, who created us.

A good friend and also homegrown kid, Roberta Cruz, wrote a short story describing her thoughts on the changes we're experiencing in our neighborhood:

I have never seen something burning up close. The other day, however, while I was making lasagna for some good friends, I burned myself. It wasn't too bad but as the days went by a part of my skin charred and wrinkled. The more time passed the stranger it looked, soon it began to peel and I realized that my skin was literally shedding off the burned parts. And although luckily for me the old skin will be replaced by a new layer underneath, the same can't be said for very much else. Think of paper, or matches . . . or houses. All things that cannot be revived.

And sadly my house is not the first to be set ablaze. Sandra Cisneros, one of my favorite writers, said this about her house in south side Chicago: "the house we live in is on fire and the people we love are burning." If only she knew that she took the words right out of my heart. I too feel the burning sting of the flames every time I read about the plans for my street. I feel my lungs tighten as the smoke slowly suffocates every time I overhear the conversations about making room for improvements in my neighborhood, but improvements that won't be for me or the houses like mine.

And I can't help but think "What will become of my house once it's all burned out? What will be left?" I wonder if we will walk through the rubbish like children searching for at least one thing, anything still familiar. We will think "Was anything saved from the fire?" And will it even matter if there was?

And it's true my house has wooden creaky floors that to you sound like noise but to me sound like the strums of guitarras and the drumming of tamboras that my mom danced to on Saturdays. My house is filled with voices that to you sound like gibberish, but to me is the language of wisdom, passed-down jokes and love. It has an old kitchen that to you require serious renovations but if you only knew all the illnesses sancochos and tés from that kitchen have cured. If after you've displaced an entire culture and removed every inch of what it was, will you simply build a new house and move on?

Maybe you will. But not without knowing the stories of my house first. After you've heard and felt the stories of my home, then if you still feel free to continue to watch it burn, that's on you; but I assure you, watching a house burn is probably much harder to do if something in the house was yours too. And maybe it's not your fault, because maybe your whole life letting things burn has always been easier than putting fires out.

No one ever loves alone, no one heals alone, no one learns alone. Learning, livening and healing are all part of journey that we share. In life, its relationship that transform.

—Unknown

CHAPTER 2

Make Homes, Build Families: *Entre Familia*

"New York City is great for many reasons," said the tour guide, in a calm but convincing voice. "Perhaps New York City is great because of its architecture, or perhaps its art and culture. Or perhaps New York City is great because of its history. While those may be true, New York City is great primarily because every day she shatters whatever you thought you knew about her."

These were thoughtful words from Mick, our tour guide around Manhattan on the city cruise line. My buddy Alex, a native New Yorker but living in Atlanta at the time, was back home for a weekend celebrating his birthday. His wife had put together a guys' weekend that included this tour.

Mick was partially right. New York City does shatter whatever you thought you knew about her. She's always changing, always moving. Hardly anything ever stays the same in New York City. As one historian said, "New York is never finished."[1] Perhaps that's why she never sleeps. But even though all that is true, New York City also reminds you that some things you think about her *are* true, such as her density, busyness, and diversity.

Cities—their rhythms, history, dreams, values, and fears—are storytellers by nature. When we sit and watch the local news, analyze the city's budget, and consider her elected public officials; when we sit at our children's parent association meeting and look around the room; when we visit our city's museums—all of these things tell us the story of the city. Jumping on the A train during rush hour isn't just a ride to work with several hundred fellow neighbors—it's NYC's version of story time in the morning. The everyday and seemingly insignificant activities of our lives tell more about who we are, what we love, and what we fear than we could explain if we were directly asked how we see ourselves.

One aspect of Gotham's story is the dynamic of family life in the city. (Gotham is a name given to New York City by fiction novelist Washington Irving in the 1800s.) The truth is that families—their presence or their absence, their health or their lack of health, and so on—will have a huge effect on the future of our cities, especially as related to their spiritual climate.

A Walk in the Lower

I remember walking through one of Lower Manhattan's neighborhoods on a sunny September afternoon. As I walked through the community with my wife and two children, we watched the crowds pleasantly, casually walking along. The passersby drank their iced coffees and enjoyed conversations with their friends. But after a few minutes of walking, I realized something that I would have probably missed if I hadn't been with my family—there weren't many children around. I didn't hear much crying, or whining, or asking for things that they probably weren't going to get. Although we saw a ton of people, we didn't see frustrated parents who wanted to enjoy the day just like everyone else but couldn't because either their children had missed their nap or they had too many things to carry and not enough hands to enjoy an iced coffee like the rest of us. We thought to ourselves, *Where are the families?*

We weren't angry or bitter; we just found it interesting. I am aware that there are heaps of reasons (as my New Zealand friends would say) why parents grow frustrated and impatient with their children—selfishness, mixed-up priorities, and idolatry, just to name a few. But could there be external reasons why, in our Sunday afternoon experience, my family felt lonely in our own city? (I'm including my kids here, because they have feelings too.) Admittedly, it was an isolated moment, and maybe it was unique to that particular neighborhood, yet the experience taught us a few things.

As I considered how New York City was born, I asked myself how the city's early history could help shape my understanding of family life in the city today. But it wasn't until I was watching *New York: A Documentary Film* by Ric Burns, that I realized more profoundly the connection between the two. In the documentary, while discussing the relationship between the first Dutch settlers and the Lenape tribe that already lived on the island, historian John Steele Gordon said, "New York was founded for no other reason than to make a buck!"[2] The documentary highlights the business transaction between the Lenape Indians and the Dutch West Indian Company, who bought the island of Manhattan for around $600. Other people explored new land for religious freedom, but some say that the Dutch people's motivation for exploration was to make a profit and outdo their rivals, the English. From being our country's first capital city (although that isn't often taught in school), to becoming the home for the first national bank, to having the third-largest and busiest harbor in the world, to giving birth to the largest stock exchange in the world, New York City is the undisputed epicenter of influence. And although we are the mother of many great and glorious influences, we have decided to lead with consumerism—the art of self-glory.

There is plenty we can say about our city's history, but here's what we cannot afford to miss: the commercial culture has been the love interest of New York from its inception. If there is a thread that runs deep through the fabric of our city—from its origins to its current reality—it is our singular focus on consuming as much as we can while never putting that consumption in jeopardy. This may not be true of all New Yorkers, but it is certainly the climate that New York presents to any explorer. Whether you personally share this mentality or not, you have to deal with this weather if you're going to live in this city. And quite frankly, every one of us will live out that climate to one degree or another.

Thanks for the nosebleed, Rich, but what does all this history have to do with families in the city? Well, do you remember my Sunday afternoon with my family? Do you remember us feeling lonely?

In this kind of environment, families are more than likely to, at best, endure the city for a couple of years and then quickly move elsewhere at the first opportunity. Whatever space they vacate when they leave is typically filled by people who can enjoy pleasant, child-free strolls and hangouts. At least this seems to be the trend right now. Cities generally are not set up to prioritize families and the rhythms that families need to thrive and flourish. When families don't find the emotional and spiritual room to exist, along with all of their new—and, thus, often difficult—dynamics, they either decay or transition out of the city. If families can't find a space where the things they celebrate are also what the community celebrates, loneliness sets in rather quickly and they again begin to decay or phase out of the city. The deceptive thing is that in a city like New York, there are droves of people around you—but little intimacy. Close to 350,000 people live within a one-mile radius in my neighborhood alone.

My story was forged here. It's the one thing about me over which I had absolutely no control. Had I been born a year earlier, I would've been an immigrant from the Dominican Republic along with my parents. But they decided to come to the States in 1983 instead, so I was born right here. And what I'm learning is that loving my city well, and loving it more purposefully, calls me to make homes and build families. So what does it mean to do that, and why is that important to the way we live in the city?

Seventy Years!

I'm reminded of Jeremiah, one of God's prophets. God would call on Jeremiah, share an intimate message with him, and then tell him to share that message with the nation of Israel. A lot of folks describe Jeremiah as the weeping prophet—depressive and kind of suicidal at times. He lamented because God used him as his mouthpiece quite often, for close to fifty years, in fact. But despite being used often by God, Jeremiah frequently wasn't heard by the people. And not being heard can become discouraging. (Where are my parents of young kids?!)

In any case, Jeremiah writes to the people of God while they are exiles in Babylon, a foreign land:

> Find wives for yourselves, and have sons and daughters. Find wives for your sons and give your daughters to men in marriage so that they may bear sons and daughters. Multiply there; do not decrease. Pursue the well-being of the city I have deported you to. Pray to the LORD on its behalf, for when it thrives, you will thrive. (Jer. 29:6–7)

It's interesting to read this in its full context. Before this chapter, another supposed prophet tried lifting the spirits of the people by telling them that their captivity would quickly come to an end. This false prophet even went as far as demonstrating his message by breaking the wooden yoke—a heavy, enslaving mechanism around the neck—that Jeremiah had put on himself. The false prophet did that to symbolically oppose Jeremiah's message and to demonstrate that God would destroy their captivity rather than prolong it. But this was not God's message to his people. In fact, in verses 6 and 7, God shows us the opposite. The people will not be freed from their captivity for another seventy years, so they might as well unpack and get comfortable. In other words, God believed that the best thing to offer the powerful metropolis of Babylon was not the absence of family, but the presence and flourishing growth of his family.

In reading this biblical passage, my attention was drawn not only to the seventy years that God planned for his people to be exiles in this city, but also to the vision he had for them while they were to be living there. God envisioned that his people would not merely exist there, but would also passionately pursue the welfare of Babylon because "when it thrives, you will thrive." In other words, we aren't merely to take up space until things change or God comes to finally establish his city on earth. We're not called to be residents, but neighbors. We're called to hope deeply, imagine creatively, and take ownership of the places God puts us.

Can we really believe that leading an anti-consumer life in a primarily consumer-driven city is not only sustainable, but satisfying? Can we really believe that elevating family values—such as sacrifice, selfless living, and investment without return (at least not the return you were expecting)—can influence a city to adopt those values as its own? Do we really believe that these values are what our cities need?

When Jeremiah talks about welfare, he's talking about wholeness. And when we talk about wholeness, we imply that something is missing, broken, and not as it should be. What we're saying is that families are becoming the invisible demographic, and I wonder how paralyzing that is to the growth and enrichment of our cities and neighborhoods. I wonder what we will forfeit if we don't come to value families and the dynamics with which they live much more highly than we do right now.

When family is missing from the heart of our cities and neighborhoods, it seems to me that we forfeit a few things. First of all, we forfeit our *dependence*. At first glance, this might not sound very convincing, but for any city or any neighborhood to overcome grave obstacles and thrive, we have to first feel like we need each other. I think of my particular neighborhood, Washington Heights, as an example of this. In the early and mid-nineties, the residents pulled together to overcome some of the darkest obstacles any New York City neighborhood had ever seen. Hispanics, blacks, Jewish neighbors, and Irish neighbors all realized that it would take their collaborative efforts to transform Washington Heights from being the capital of crack cocaine to being one of the safest and most family-friendly neighborhoods in our city.

Yet the truer fabric of cities is not dependence, but rather *independence*. Often the narrative that cities push on us is that our only chance of making it is on our own. Again, I think of my own community. What has always been, in my experience, a family-friendly community is now morphing into an attractive place for single, affluent, apartment-sharing residents, which is slowly making families feel less and less welcome. Again, I'm not opposed to diversifying. I want the community to be more welcoming, but certainly not at the cost of families, which are a pillar in the growth of communities. Consider a CEO or someone who is highly accomplished. When they climb to the top, what we typically hear—aside from some courteous thank-yous—is that they have been entirely responsible for their own success. Although that may be true, I'm certain that many of them would gladly trade their achievements for a greater sense of family and intimacy—which was probably absent in their journey to the top.

There is something uniquely special, and of course convicting, about watching a child climb on their dad, mom, *tío*, or *tía*, just to reach the countertop for their favorite cereal. Or even something as simple as your son or nephew calling you over and asking you to walk along the monkey bars with him so that he can reach the end safely, because it's his first time trying that. Or even watching a mom at the park feeding her baby while she gives her preteen a dollar to buy an Icee. That picture depicts the need that we all have and shows us the value of having this demographic segment around. There is a reason why mentorship programs are such a success and why their absence is so devastating. This is at the heart of what God intended for families—that they would serve as reminders that we need each other. Our moments of deepest love, joy, celebration, struggle, victory, and forgiveness all occur in the presence of the people closest to us. God leaves no room for mistaking his vision behind the "one anothers" in his story—"Love one another . . . Teach and admonish one another . . . Carry one another's burdens . . . Pray for one another . . . Serve one another" (John 15:12; Col. 3:16 (NIV); Gal. 6:2; James 5:16; Gal. 5:13). It's healthy to admit need, because it's a fresh reminder of our unique and divine design. We were created to need. Our need drives us to God, who offers satisfaction for "all your needs according to his riches in glory in Christ Jesus" (Phil. 4:19).

Growth is another benefit that we seem to forfeit when families are missing from the heart of our cities and neighborhoods. Again, this might sound a bit extreme, but I think it's worth exploring. "Rich, do you mean to tell me that growth is possible only through family?" I couldn't answer yes to that question with a clear conscience, so my answer is no, but with a big *but*. Family is not the only means for growth, but it is a huge component. Family often offers us tension, which is good for our growth because it flies in the face of personal comfort. I've learned, over the last few years, how damaging and stifling unreasonable comfort is. Marriage and parenting have shown me how deeply selfish I am, and how debilitating my selfishness is to me and my family. Before marriage and having kids, I lived my life in spiritual and emotional safety. And in many ways, my goal during that season was to steer clear of anything that would put that safety in jeopardy or make me vulnerable to personal loss.

We've all seen it—on the train, on the bus, or in the park. *Shoot!* Sometimes we've done it ourselves. There's the parent who's out with the group, but their child starts crying or asking for something that will inconvenience the group in some way. The parent is now confronted with the choice of either brushing the child off or considering the child's need, legitimate or not. Long before we ask questions about what we want, we're thinking through what our child needs. Although I'm not saying that parents are the only people who think this way, I am suggesting that a family environment often best sets the ground for someone to approach relationships that way. If you grew up in an environment in which you were one of many, it can be much easier for you to learn and live out sacrifice than for people who didn't grow up that way. For you, it can be much easier to be other-people-faced.

When my dad was patient.

The bottom line is that growth doesn't come from thinking about oneself. Growth comes from thinking outside of oneself. What I've learned is exactly what Jesus tells me: "If anyone wants to follow after me, let him deny himself, take up his cross, and follow me. For whoever wants to save his life will lose it, but whoever loses his life because of me will find it" (Matt. 16:24–25). We can exhaust our time, efforts, and resources to protect our own comfort, but in the end, we rob ourselves of the growth and Jesus-likeness that comes from radically thinking of others above ourselves. We rob ourselves of the opportunity to relate to Jesus in the same uniquely special way that he related to us. Our tendency will always be to protect self and, even further, to build up self. That's easy. The real work comes in loving, building up, and considering others above yourself. Quite frankly, it goes beyond just hard work—it takes faith to "die to yourself" just a little with every passing day in order to feel alive. I once heard it said this way: "Parenting is more about the parent growing up than it is about the child growing up." I'm not an expert at parenting, but it sure does feel that way.

Sacrifice is a tricky thing, ain't it? Sometimes it seems like it pushes us to go further than we thought we needed to go. Well, if that's your experience, you're in good company. The disciples of Jesus had the same experience—Peter, in particular.

Consider what Jesus tells his disciples in John 12:24–25. Jesus introduces a radical understanding on how we are to lead our lives. He says, "Truly I tell you, unless a grain of wheat falls to the ground and dies, it remains by itself. But if it dies, it produces much fruit. The one who loves his life will lose it, and the one who hates his life in this world will keep it for eternal life."

Now, forgive me, but as a *city dude*, I don't know much about planting grains of wheat. I don't know much about horticulture. But I do know a lot about egos. I do know a lot about playing on a team. I do know that there is a vast difference between what my ego wants to accomplish and what my team wants to accomplish. I know that my ego is actively working against what my team is working toward. I know that my ego and my team cannot both win. I know that the moment I step on the court, my ego—just like this grain of wheat—must die, or else I will exist by myself while impacting no one.

Jesus is challenging what the disciples thought about his mission. Jesus is saying that the journey of discipleship is marked by a commitment to living sacrificially. In Matthew 16, Jesus says something very similar, this time with Peter in the room.

I want you to put yourself in the shoes of Peter the disciple for a moment. Imagine you were raised near the Sea of Galilee, in a town filled with mixed-race people, who belong everywhere, but belong nowhere. People in your town fish for a living and, generally speaking, live simple lives. They live under an oppressive government. They are unreasonably taxed—and they can only hope for better days. Days when the promised Messiah will come and restore the nation of Israel and put an end to exploitation and oppression as they know it.

One day you meet a unique teacher. You listen to him. You see him do great signs and miracles. You see large crowds follow him around like no one else before. You take him out on your boat. You take his professional advice on fishing, even though he's a carpenter. You become a close friend and, in the end, you're convinced that this is the Messiah that your people have been waiting for. You have high expectations for him and you can't wait to see him do what you expect the Messiah to do. You can't wait till your family sees this! Then Jesus tells you, "You're right! I am the Messiah. God must've revealed that to you, but don't tell anyone yet." Then you start to wonder why. Why on God's good planet can't you tell people? This is good news, isn't it? Don't you want people to know this? But you trust him nonetheless. So you keep the news low.

But then Matthew 16:21–26 happens:

> From then on Jesus began to point out to his disciples that it was necessary for him to go to Jerusalem and suffer many things from the elders, chief priests, and scribes, be killed, and be raised the third day. Peter took him aside and began to rebuke him, "Oh no, Lord! This will never happen to you."
>
> Jesus turned and told Peter, "Get behind me, Satan! You are a hindrance to me because you are not thinking about God's concerns but human concerns."
>
> Then Jesus said to his disciples, "If anyone wants to follow after me, let him deny himself, take up his cross, and follow me. For whoever wants to save his life will lose it, but whoever loses his life because of me will find it. For what will it benefit someone if he gains the whole world yet loses his life? Or what will anyone give in exchange for his life?"

To the eyes of Peter and the disciples, Jesus wasn't making any sense. Of course, Peter knew that this journey was going to require sacrifice, but he didn't think that sacrifice was going to go this far!

What Jesus is saying to Peter and to us is that truly following him will require a considerable shift in our thinking. This is not just a challenge to think differently about what Jesus came to do, but also about what Jesus calls us to do. When Jesus redefines his own mission in light of Peter's perception, he simultaneously redefines Peter's mission and anyone who would follow him.

Another thing we forfeit when families are missing from the heart of our cities and neighborhoods is *joy*. When personal comfort is not chin-checked by the sacrificial mind-set, we begin to lose sight of the good news of Jesus. In fact, we start to believe that anything that helps build personal comfort seems like *better* news. We start looking forward to things that keep risks at bay and hold personal interest as close as possible. We look forward to things that can quench our immediate desires, because we believe that suffering in any form is far too costly. It's too costly because our joy and identity are wrapped up in what we have now, what we feel now, and who is in our lives now. The moment those things are challenged or taken away is the moment our world collapses. We say to ourselves,

I can't afford to have my life, as it is now, disturbed or shaken up, so I will protect it and build it by any means necessary.

Pursuing our own comfort communicates that there is no greater reality for our lives than the one we can experience here in this world. But that's just not true. The money we have now is not the only treasure we will ever have. The relationships we have now aren't the only intimacy we will ever experience. Even Woody Allen knows that something exists beyond our tangible reality. In a comedic way, he shows the tension of convenience and wanting to experience some other reality. As Allen says, "There is no question that there is an unseen world. The problem is how far is it from Midtown and how late is it open?"[3] The gospel of Jesus offers us something more sure than the things and relationships in whom we place our trust in this life.

Because the nature of family often pushes up against our personal comforts, a family environment has the tendency to encourage us to live for a greater reality than just our own. In a season of suffering or difficulty, Jesus becomes an advocate and helper, rather than a culprit. We're less likely to pump our fist to the sky and say, "God, this is all your fault." Instead we look up to the heavens for understanding, compassion, and rescue. "Every word of God is pure; he is a shield to those who take refuge in him" (Prov. 30:5). We begin to realize that Jesus didn't come to make our lives better or easier, but to make them meaningful. When the world is falling apart around us and reaching for our ambitions wears us down, life never loses meaning. And that's because we never lose the one who gives it to us: Jesus. Now we can begin to see that Jesus wasn't given to the world for us to enjoy a two-week vacation every December, but so "that [Jesus's] joy may be in [us] and [our] joy may be complete" (John 15:11)—never in jeopardy of fading away.

Although I know that pockets of the city still see families as valuable, my fear is that cities are moving away from embracing families. I'm afraid cities are not making families feel welcome and not considering family dynamics. So what happens? What's the move?

Well, I—for one—won't run from the city. At least not unless I get the call from the bullpen to go elsewhere. Even then, I'll have a difficult time believing that God would call me away from a city altogether. And despite some scary things about raising kids in urban centers and inner cities, I'm convinced that fighting for presence and influence here is, in large part, what the city needs. It does, however, wear you down.

It does take resolve. It does eat away at you, making hope and vision absolutely necessary for everyone in your family.

Here are some things that my family considers along the way. For starters, we confront our fears with reality, hope, and faith. For every fear we have, there's a truth that stands in opposition to it. It's true that raising kids in the city makes them more vulnerable to seeing dark things that you wish they hadn't. But it is not true that family life outside the city is void of the same kind of darkness, which is sometimes even more insidious. The common fear is that kids in the city will see drug deals on their way to school, prostitution across the street from the park, or a sea of homeless people just before reaching the bodega for a gallon of milk. And although that might not always be the case, it is the reality in many ways and at many times. I certainly lived it as a kid in this neighborhood. But shielding your kids from seeing those things doesn't keep them from the lustful thoughts they can entertain in the privacy of their own room. Shielding your kids from seeing those things doesn't keep them from living in a nice house and yet being in a broken home and feeling abandoned. Shielding your kids from seeing those things doesn't keep them from having to confront the anger that lives inside of them because of broken relationships.

Anna and my queen, Charlotte, walking out of a train station.

Almost every morning, on our walk to school, my son and I pass by a gentleman. We know he works for one of the supers on our street, because we often see him lugging carpentry and plumbing tools around. But sadly, he's in bad shape almost every morning. We greet him as we pass by, and he slurs some words back at us, reeking from the alcohol he probably guzzled down the previous night. My son once asked me, *"Papi,* why does he smell like that and why does he talk like that?"

I couldn't avoid answering his question. I couldn't avoid talking about alcohol, how to enjoy it, and how we often misuse it. I realized I couldn't avoid talking about drunkenness and sobriety. I couldn't avoid talking about how things in life often enslave us. I couldn't avoid talking about what true freedom is, and how it allows us to enjoy a good thing while not making it an ultimate thing. I realized in that moment that I couldn't avoid any of it. I had to hold my son's hand, cross the street, and offer him a response!

Although the fear is that our children might lose their innocence if they're exposed to this, the truth is that there is no innocence to lose. Instead, these moments—scary as they may seem—provide us an opportunity to have meaningful conversations with our kids. My point is that the city forces us, as parents, to be present while our children experience the world. Sin and its consequences are ugly, and although the city tries to glamorize that, parents have the unique opportunity to retell the story of the city through faith, hope, and obedience. This is precisely what God envisions when he tells Israelite parents,

> "Hear, O Israel: The LORD our God, the LORD
> is one. You shall love the LORD your God with

all your heart and with all your soul and with all your might. And these words that I command you today shall be on your heart. You shall teach them diligently to your children, and shall talk of them when you sit in your house, and when you walk by the way, and when you lie down, and when you rise." (Deut. 6:4–7 ESV)

Here's another thing that my family does along the way: we work to build relationships because they inspire rootedness. It's difficult to leave a place when you're not simply leaving an apartment or a street block, but also leaving friendships. Make friends with the *bodegero*, the clerk at the corner store. Make friends with the servers at your routine breakfast spot. Make friends with anyone you want, but be sure that a handful of those are truly meaningful friendships. In a true friendship, whether or not you see the world the same way, you deeply care for one another and find strength from your shared experiences. Let your kids forge those kinds of friendships as well.

We can all admit to the difficulty of finding and forging depth in relationships. Everything from past hurts, uncertainty, and downright pessimism gets in the way. But if we don't have these kinds of relationships, we should not be at all surprised that living a transient life is easier than committing to people. We should not be at all surprised if loneliness follows us around more than friendships do. We should not be at all surprised if any small difference drives us to another church, rather than allowing the differences to shape us into a stronger body. As I've heard said, "When things don't go our way, we go shopping." If it's been an emotionally difficult week at home, then you're sure to find an H&M or Nike shopping bag somewhere in our house. It's just easier to move past something than to confront it. Yet here's what I'm learning: as Christians we want to influence the world, but we often fail to build the relationship and compassion that precede influence. Compassion and relationship will always precede influence.

Paul's letter to the Thessalonians helps illustrate my point. He says,

> Nor did we seek glory from people, whether from you or from others, though we could have made demands as apostles of Christ. But we were gentle among you, like a nursing mother taking care of her own children. So, being affectionately desirous of you, we were ready to share with you not only the gospel of God but

also our own selves, because you had become very dear to us. (1 Thess. 2:6–8 ESV)

Third, we raise our children to live in the tension of a world that they ought to love, but a world that will often reject them because of Jesus. This is difficult for anyone, let alone children. But if we're going to inspire our world to faith, then raising children who first see themselves as citizens of God's kingdom is important. Although both of our kids have their own unique experiences, we're realizing that they're both wrestling through some variation of three major life questions. These are questions that we, as adults, often ask ourselves. First is the question of identity: "Who am I?" Second is the question of security: "Can I trust my world?" And third is the question of morality: "How should I live?" This may sound farfetched, but these questions are the very reason that we're all explorers. This is the very reason my son, at two years old, used to inch his way over to the stove, turn his head slightly in my direction, and slowly reach over to touch the stove. He was curious. He wanted to see if it would burn, or whether my reprimand from the previous time was enough to let him slide this time.

This is why, even now, I'm wrestling to know what it means to be a second-generation Dominican in America. Can you imagine some of our conversations with our kids—who are Dominican, Peruvian, and Puerto Rican? I'll tell you one thing: those conversations can get loud! These questions are also why, as a teenager, I tried weed in a bathroom stall just to see how I would feel, or even how my conscience would lead me. This is why my son sometimes comes home from school overwhelmed with worry, because of how his friends might react if they saw him praying over his food at lunchtime. We are explorers by nature. We're curious. And our responsibility isn't to condemn or, even worse, extinguish that curiosity, but rather to guide it and lead it to the God of the Bible, who rewards curiosity and searching with his presence. "The LORD is near all who call out to him, all who call out to him in integrity" (Ps. 145:18).

Part of the responsibility of parenting or mentoring is to help children decipher their actions—why they behave in the way they do, why they long for mischief or attention, and why they find more comfort among dudes from the corner than they do at home. We do, say, and think things because we're in search of something ultimately significant and because we're curious about ultimate meaning. We try things. Please understand me. I'm not advocating for a flippant style of parenting or mentorship, where we let them learn primarily by their mistakes. What I am saying is that investment in parenting or mentorship, as I'm learning, involves not flipping out when your child does something that you wish he or she hadn't. Investment involves dialogue. It involves teaching and instructing, of course, but it also involves patience and grace and love when your instructions and insights aren't the same as your children's convictions—just yet.

It should not surprise us that avoiding meaningful conversations with our children—about identity, security, and morality—will leave them not only incapacitated, but also uninspired. And raising uninspired people is the worst thing you can offer your city. What if, instead, we saw our children, as Psalm 127:3 calls us to do, as "a heritage . . . a reward"? It's interesting to see the word *heritage* here. I'm reminded of our ethnic heritage—something that we could never undo even if we wanted to. I can travel anywhere in the world, and I will always travel with my Dominican heritage. I can't simply check my heritage with the airline and jump on the plane without it, hoping it will arrive at my final destination with me. We've all been on a trip or two where our bag didn't make it all the way. We know the feeling. *This* is not *that*. Instead, the word *heritage* is used here in the context of property, more specifically an inalienable property. In other words, this is a heritage that we cannot disown.

Yet sadly, there are many children who feel disowned in my city alone. New York City has about 59,000 homeless people running through the shelter system,[4] and 23,692 of them are children.[5] New York City has 10,604 kids in the foster care system,[6] and 8,663 kids are named in open child abuse or neglect investigations.[7] These numbers should alarm us. These numbers should convince us all the more of the need for healthy family presence and influence in our cities. These numbers should drive us to become big brothers and big sisters, mentors, and *tíos and tías* to our neighborhood kids.

In the end, I'm realizing that my deep love for Uptown has its roots in my deep love for family. In fact, all of us long for this deep love of family. My hope is that men will lead with strength, confidence, and tenderness because at the cross Jesus redefined strength. That women will be valued and honored because at the cross Jesus won back our dignity. That children will be cared for and invested in because at the cross Jesus made it clear that we were worth the investment. But for men to lead well, for women to be valued and honored, and for children to be cared for and invested in—for families to impact a city—we have to embrace that city. We have to make that city home. This is a tall task for many like myself, who wrestle with the concept of *home,* because we're not a part of the dominant culture.

Living in the Hyphen

Furcy Pérez. That's my dad's name. For years, my dad worked as a porter in an office building on Fifth Avenue. After his retirement, I made it a point to spend more time with him. We'd go out for lunch, hang at the mall, or watch games at his house. In a recent hang at the diner near my house, we talked for hours about our past, our families, and our future. Growing up, it's hard to imagine being an adult and having serious conversations with your parents. Nevertheless, we did, and it was refreshing. But at a lull in the conversation, I reluctantly asked, "Oye, Pah, are you considering moving back to the Dominican Republic?" He scoffed and said, "No, *muchacho. Yo no vuelvo pa'llá.*" In other words, "There's no reason to go back."

Although his response prompted a deep sigh of relief from me, it also got my gears turning about a few things. If there's anything I've learned over the course of three decades, it's that immigrants in this country live with a unique tension between national pride and foreign hope. In other words, they deeply love the place from which they came, but the promise of America is more compelling. My dad left the Dominican Republic not because he wasn't proud or didn't love his country, but because he desired something better for himself and his children. He loves his Dominican culture and heritage. But he left there to establish for himself and his children a life that would offer more than he saw possible in his home country. So my dad's response was interesting, because it was as if he was saying, "I'm thinking about not going back, because I'm not sure if I fit there anymore."

The more time I spent with my dad, the more it seemed to me that the immigrant experience in this country is like the foster care experience. In both situations, you have little if any relationship with your biological parents, but neither do you feel like your foster parents are your family or that their home is your home.

As I talked with my dad, I realized how lonely that tension was. There were so many great things in his life—family, health, and faith—but in many other ways there was ambivalence, a kind of uncertainty about where he fit in. My dad, perhaps like every immigrant, was growing more and more hungry for home, the place where he knew without a shadow of a doubt that he was with family in an environment of deep and constant refreshment. Although he might get that at times with family and friends, it's hardly the immigrants'—or from their perspective, the foreigners'—experience in this country. In an effort to capture the immigrants' experience, Justo González, a Cuban-American history professor, says this:

> The literal exiles live in the ambiguity between gratitude and anger. We are grateful, because this country has offered us a refuge others did not. But at the same time we are angry, mostly for two reasons: first, because many of us are coming to the bitter realization that even though we have given up the countries of our birth, we shall end our days as exiles, as people who live in a land that is not theirs, that welcomes them up to a point and then shuts the door. Second, we are angry because we are becoming increasingly aware of the degree to which the United States, the land of our refuge, is also the land that created our need for exile in the first place.[8]

This is only my dad's experience; I would hate to assume that this is every immigrant's experience. Yet I wonder how many immigrants, foreigners, strangers, marginalized people, and poor people are walking our neighborhoods and feeling like they don't belong. Feeling as though there's no place they can confidently call home. Feeling uncertain of the commitment other people have to them.

El Tun-tún

My dad was big on music. Especially after long days of work and on the weekends. I saw all sorts of sound equipment come through the apartment. He had the 8-track cassette player. Then he had the vinyl player—I know, it seems backward, but it was only later in his life that my dad grew a passion for collecting vinyls. Then, about a decade after they first hit the stores, my dad brought home a sleek black Fisher 24-CD player. *Wepa!* This was big. Really big. I remember being excited mostly about the fact that it had this little window you could peek into and see the CDs in their slots, rotating when they had been called on by the controller or the buttons on the player. It was as if each CD had its own cozy place and the player was the home for all of them. The player was digital too. Up to that point, our family hadn't seen much of the digital world. Needless to say, those twenty-four CDs became everything to our home. My dad had over a hundred CDs, most of them stacked in those CD towers we got at the Dyckman electronics store (which was always just known as "the electronic store on Dyckman" because they were never creative enough to call it anything but Dyckman Electronics—brilliant!).

At any rate, those twenty-four CDs made the pick because they were the most listened to, the best to clean the apartment to, or were recently purchased by *papi* and he was giving them the two-week test of how they sounded *en el sistema*. My dad's sound system was impressive, and as a result, coveted. He wasn't a tyrant about it—that's not his personality. But he was always very clear about our use of the CD player, which felt more like a prohibition. He wanted to ensure that his twenty-four were always in the player, and even more particularly, that each one was in its proper slot. Because of course, he had the albums and their slot number memorized. This made it easier for him to wake up on a day off, go to his controller, press number twenty-one and rock out *Jossie Esteban Y La Patrulla 15*! Yeah, I know. He got straight to it on Saturdays. No runway. No easing into the music. No slow ballad. Just straight *merengue*!

I'll never forget the day I decided to mess around with his faithful, black "golden" box. It was a day my dad was working a double shift at the garage, which meant he wouldn't get home until much later, perhaps until after I was in bed. I was fourteen years old, in my freshman year of high school, and drooling over my new CD: *Volume 2 . . . Hard Knock Life* by Jay-Z. I thought about it for a bit, but not for long. Then I did it. I took out number twelve in the player and slid *Hard Knock Life* in through the opening that always made me think I was putting a giant coin in the music vending machine. I rocked out to the whole album. I think it was the first time I heard any of my music in the system. It was euphoric. Listening to hip-hop in my dad's sound system was part of what fueled my love for the genre in the years to come. But here's the thing—I enjoyed the music so much, I forgot to put Wilfrido Vargas back into the number twelve slot. Jay-Z kept the slot warm overnight. Next morning vibes come around. My dad wakes up. Makes his *avena*. Butters his *tostada*. And of course, he grabs his controller with the urge to listen to Wilfrido Vargas—of all records, he summons number twelve from the carousel of CDs on his controller. "Wah wah wah!" pierced through the system at full volume, resembling the *Shaft* theme song. It was the guitar sounds that gave you an idea of what a boomerang would sound like. The note played then came back to you. Then came in the kick drum, "tun, tún!" It was Jay-Z's "Reservoir Dogs" playing!

My dad was in such shock he didn't even know what buttons to press to shut it off. All I heard next were the thumps of his footsteps rushing to my room. Each step louder than the one before it. He flung the door open, and as he glared at me he said, *"muchacho! ven quítame el 'tun-tún!' e'te!"*

My dad had always called hip-hop *"el tun-tún"* primarily because of the heavy kick drums and 808s in the production. I was just glad he didn't rip my head off for messing with his baby! But here's the irony: after I took Jay out and helped him get Wilfrido Vargas back in, my dad cooled off from the shock and played "Jardín de Rosas." It was Wilfrido Vargas' catchy merengue that had two rap verses in it! It was Wilfrido's creative attempt at leveraging a genre that was, quite frankly, finding its way into all cultures and music. Hip-hop was permeating my world. I sat in my room thinking through my dad's reaction to "Reservoir Dogs" and hearing Wilfrido Vargas rapping in his merengue, and

I suddenly realized how that moment would begin to define much of my experience thereafter.

I'm Dominican. I'm American. My heritage has influenced me to love mangu, merengue, and lively (nice way of saying "loud") family get-togethers. Yet at the same time, and perhaps in equally significant ways, I've grown to love pizza, English slang, and Nas' *Illmatic*. It was a great day at school when the cafeteria was serving cheeseburgers with french fries. But on the rowdy BX19 bus ride home with friends, I couldn't wait to sink my teeth in the *arroz blanco* with two *huevos fritos, encebollado,* and ketchup for good measure that my pops would sometimes have ready for us. At school we'd have lively debates about Big L's rap mixtape and whether or not it cemented his place as an underground rap legend. Yet some of my most memorable moments are at family parties dancing to *Periódico De Ayer* by Hector Lavoe with tía Martha.

But perhaps more complex than just foods and music, the tension of my Dominican-American experience is lived in ways that go beyond what just anyone can see. For my eyes only, so to speak. It often feels like the tension becomes most challenging in the world of my mind and heart. The way I process and see the world.

Take, for example, speaking Spanish. For those of us who are native-born Hispanics (U.S.-born kids of immigrant parents), we just didn't think much about speaking Spanish outside our family. Even growing up in a neighborhood like Washington Heights where the obvious majority was Hispanic, as a kid you almost avoided speaking Spanish. *"Hick!"* They yelled across the room when my friend Justin was caught laughing and talking to Milagros the lunch lady in Spanish. Of course, it was done in humor. But that might be the point. Speaking Spanish was mocked. Something to laugh and poke fun at. Any slight display of speaking Spanish or doing "Spanish" things immediately transported you to the backwoods, country-side, and *fincas* of your parents' native country. And you've only visited twice in fifteen years!

English is the language we spoke in school. It's the language we spoke with our friends. It's the language we learned math, writing, and science, and explored the arts in. Our critical thinking was developed in English. The way we process conflicts and challenges is in English with English concepts leading us. We more often make connections and associations with life in New York City than we do *Santo Domingo*. I know about *novelas* like *Dos Mujeres, Un Camino,* and

Marimar, but what really drew me to the screen were TV shows like *Family Matters*, *Full House*, and *The Fresh Prince of Bel-Air*. My English vocabulary was much more polished than my Spanish vocabulary. If I'm entirely honest—and this is no indictment on my love for my heritage—it often felt like speaking Spanish was just something I gave effort to because I knew my parents weren't going to engage me in English. Speaking Spanish, in the mind of many native-born Hispanics, was for the privacy of home. Its importance was casual at best.

Our immigrant parents often enforced this way of thinking. Sure, they wanted us to remember who we are. We're Hispanic. That was never in question. Yet they also wanted us to become *"un profesional."* But becoming a professional to them meant becoming a doctor. A lawyer. Someone in government. But you couldn't become *"un profesional"* without doing well in school. And you couldn't do well in school without mastering English—the language school is offered to you in.

I remember all those *"wait till we get home"* looks I got from my mom at parent-teacher meetings. The teacher would tell her how I was underperforming, not reaching my potential in class. I know that in part those looks came from her anger. She was frustrated that I would embarrass her in front of others with my behavior. But I knew that she was also frustrated with the reality that I wasn't taking advantage of the opportunities to "progress" in the ways my parents had sacrificed for. To master life in America and thrive in ways they didn't have an opportunity to. And speaking Spanish, in their mind and ultimately ours, just wasn't important to the journey of progress. In some small, but perhaps inherent way, we thought speaking Spanish slowed us down.

If our Spanish is merely used for domestic and menial day-to-day tasks and not in complex, creative, and emotional environments, we run the risk of seeing it as nonessential or perhaps an enemy to growth and progress. And perhaps the greater danger is that we would see Spanish *speakers* not only as foreigners, but with disdain. As antithetical to achievement as we define here in America. Those with accents are looked down on. Those not educated in the American school system as insignificant and, thus, cast off.

On one side of the tension, I had a group of people making sure I wasn't too Spanish because it meant less opportunity for progress in this country. On the other side, to my family in the Dominican Republic, I was *"el Dominican Joe." "Ese muchacho e' gringo!"* my *tías* and *tíos* would say when we visited the Dominican Republic, *"A él le gusta el tun-tún y los pantalones grandes."* I was keenly aware that although Dominican ran in my veins, I wasn't Dominican in the deepest sense. To my family back in the Dominican Republic I was a "partial foreigner," as Justo González would call it. And yet, even more, on the other side of the tension, I knew I wasn't American in the deepest sense either. I knew that in a real way when, in eighth grade, I was bussed down to Stuyvesant High School in the upper-class Chelsea area of Manhattan. Some friends and I from Harlem were the only black and brown students in the entire program.

This isn't a case for why we should advocate for bilingual programs in our schools, although we can easily take it there. This is more to highlight the tension of those that live with a mixed reality—a *remezcla,* as we would say in our circles. Or what Daniel Rodriguez describes as *"living in the hyphen."* The in-between space of our worlds.

The tension can often produce some really scary things. You often feel like you don't belong. Anywhere. You are, as my *primo* Mario would say, *"ni de aquí, ni de allá."* Or *"Tú eres como el miércoles: tú 'ta en el medio!*" You are neither here nor there. You feel as if you have no real home with any one group.

You feel like you're not *pure* enough. Pure in the sense that you're not enough of one thing. You're too much a mixture of different things all at once. In conversations or through experiences, you realize that for some you're too black, you're too brown, you're too loud, you speak too much Spanish, you listen to too much hip-hop, you think too much about your family, you don't think of yourself enough, you're considering too many things, you're too much about one side and not enough about the other sides.

Justo González captures the tension of living the *remezcla*, the mixed reality, well when he says, "there's always a sense of belonging and yet not belonging, of being both fish and fowl and therefore fish to the fowl, and fowl to the fish; but also able to understand the fish as no fowl can, and the fowl like no fish can."[9]

Living the *remezcla* is living in a tension that has the power to either devastate us or help us to harness the great power and influence of how we've been created. As a Christian, I've not often seen the ways that the Bible captures my experience. Not many have helped me to see the ways the Bible affirms a *remezcla* identity. Yet this reality is not foreign to those we read about in the story of the Bible.

San Pablo

Take Saul of Tarsus—or *San Pablo*—as an example. I'll be frank, as long I've been taught the Bible, Saul has always seemed intimidating to me. He's often taught as this fearless, purebred, zealous, model believer. He seemed inaccessible to me. As if I really couldn't measure up to that level of zeal for God, his Word, and his people. Don't get me wrong—Saul is a hero of the faith. Someone worth following. He knew it himself: *"Imitate me, as I also imitate Christ"* (1 Cor. 11:1, emphasis mine). But what I came to learn is that Saul wasn't as inaccessible as he seemed to be. I could certainly find my story in Saul's. The hyphen was there, woven into his life as much as it was in mine.

The first clue is "Tarsus." Saul is from Tarsus. This might not be as clear to us today, but Tarsus was a Greco-Roman city. This meant that while it's true that Saul was Jewish—born in the tribe of Benjamin, received the best Jewish education—he was also a Hellenist. Saul was Greek; he spoke Greek. That's significant, because it meant that as a Hellenistic Jew, he wasn't fully received by the larger, Hebraic,

Aramaic-speaking Jewish community in Jerusalem. Those of an ethnically mixed reality—those living the *remezcla* like Saul—were often looked at with disdain by Hebraic Jews in Jerusalem. The Hebrews perceived the Hellenistic Jews as a mixed race with mixed blood, mixed commitment. *They couldn't possibly keep the law of God as closely and faithfully as we do,* thought the Hebraic Jews. These groups saw the law of the Old Testament and the role of the temple differently. Hellenistic Jews like Saul were not so easily embraced by Hebrews. They were considered second-class. Acts 6:1 is an example of this sort of negligence: "In those days, as the disciples were increasing in number, there arose a complaint by the Hellenistic Jews against the Hebraic Jews that their widows were being overlooked in the daily distribution [of food]." Like these Hellenistic Jews, Saul and others of mixed realities perhaps lived in the pressures of not being fully received by the Jewish community.

The second clue is Saul's name change. According to Acts 13:9 Saul was "also called Paul." Historically, I've always chalked that name change up to his experience with Jesus on the road to Damascus. It's where he was knocked off his horse by Jesus' boomin' voice and his trip to Damascus is repurposed. He was on his way with the purpose of opposing those Jews following Jesus. Now he's going to Damascus to join their mission. Paul is his new name after encountering Jesus on that dusty and fateful road. But then I realized that Luke continues to call him Saul all the way up until Acts 13 . . . four chapters after that experience! Paul, I came to realize, is not his "I met Jesus; now I live for Jesus" name. Paul is his Roman name. Romans typically had three names. Their first name, their last name, and the name their close circles called them. That's like your cousin Federicko Constatino Velasquez, but your family and friends know him as "Kiko." Well, sort of like that. Saul was Paul's Jewish name. That's what in some ways kept him connected to Jewish culture. That name helped him push up against the already negative perception Hebraic Jews had of him. He was Saul. *"Hey guys! I'm Saul! Named after our first king! I'm Jewish just like you!"* Could you imagine the pride Saul walked around with knowing that he had the name of his people's first king? More than that, he was from the same tribe as King Saul!

It's no surprise, then, that Saul was leading the cause against these "rebel" Hellenistic Jews following the way of the rebel Rabbi, Jesus. Saul perhaps thought to himself, *We already have our ethnically mixed reality working against us; we certainly don't need these rebels widening the gap between us and the Hebrews!* None of this is to say that Saul wasn't genuinely zealous for his Jewish tradition. This doesn't mean that Saul didn't want to preserve the Old Testament law. However, this does mean that zeal wasn't the only thing at play. What I came to realize is that "Saul agreed with putting [Stephen] to death" and "was still breathing threats and murder against the disciples of the Lord" (Acts 8:1; 9:1) perhaps because in the tension of his mixed reality as Roman, Greek, and Jew, Saul decided to side with what was closest to the religious center of his time—the Hebraic Jews. In his mind, they were closest to God. They were closest to truth. They were closest to tradition. Perhaps Saul's persecution of the church was motivated as much by his search for identity and belonging as it was by his zeal for the Jewish faith and tradition. Everything about Saul/Paul captures the hyphenated experience that I know well as a Dominican-American.

Yet Paul is not the only one.

The Humble Condition of Mary

Mary, the Galilean mother of Jesus, shares the same experience. After hearing the news that she would give birth to Jesus, it's important to note that she wasn't initially excited. She was concerned and afraid. Concerned that her already marginalized place in society would grow to be more marginalized by this "illegitimate" pregnancy. But once the angel reassures her that she isn't losing screws in her head and that this was God's doing, in perfect musical fashion, she breaks into song. And just like some of your favorite jams, Mary's lyrics knock hard! Mary does in her song what perhaps in some ways Nina Simone and Kendrick Lamar and Lin-Manuel have sought to do in their generations and in their genres. Mary is able to capture the moment of her time and her experiences, and with her words she looks upward, prays for divine intervention, and praises God for his provisions.

In her song, Mary gives us the primary reason that she sings to God. In Luke 1:46–48 she says, "My soul praises the greatness of the Lord, and my spirit rejoices in God my Savior, because he has looked with favor on the humble condition of his servant."

The phrase "humble condition" is interesting because it means a few things. As we know, the Bible wasn't written in English, or Spanish. It was written in Hebrew, Aramaic, and Greek. These languages often call for a family of words in English in order to faithfully capture all that the words try to communicate. In the case of Mary's lyrics, "humble condition" means poor, miserable, insignificant, and captive.

In other words, Mary is keenly aware of where she falls in the social strata of her time. There's no question that Mary sits at the margins of society and it has caused her to feel miserable, unimportant, and even trapped in a cycle of poverty much like the marginalized groups of our time—communities of color and immigrants, for example.

But Mary wasn't just poor. Mary was also a woman in a society whose perception of women was reckless at best and oppressive at worst. Mary was a woman in a society whose laws would often leave women among the most vulnerable—much like widows and orphans.

But it gets more challenging for her. Mary was also Galilean.

Galilee was the region of Israel that historically was home to the largest population of racially intermixed people. When King Solomon tried to make friends with one of the non-Jewish nations around Israel, we read in 1 Kings 9:11 that he did so by handing over twenty towns in the region of Galilee to their king. This created a society in that region that was even more racially intermixed.

All of this seems to create a unique experience for those coming out from that region. Galileans often found themselves in this middle, somewhat intermediate, and ambiguous space. On one hand, it was a space where Hebrews would perceive them as not entirely Jewish. Galileans weren't fully received as "one of them," and were often treated with disdain. They were second class among other Jews.

It was this sort of perception of Galileans that birthed sarcastic and pessimistic statements. Hebrews would say of them, "Can anything good come out of Nazareth [town in Galilee]?" (John 1:46). They would make statements dripping with doubt. A perfect example of this occurred during the ministry of Jesus. While the Pharisees were arguing about his legitimacy as a prophet, one Pharisee stood up in defense of him, asking that he be given a fair trial with an opportunity to speak. The rest of the Pharisees replied: "You aren't from Galilee too, are you? Investigate and you will see that no prophet arises from Galilee" (John 7:52). It was the kind of disdain that led them to make statements that associated Galileans with criminality. Peter is a prime example of this. After he had twice denied his association with Jesus during his very sketchy trial, someone in the crowd said to Peter, "You really are one of them, since even your [Galilean] accent gives you away" (Matt. 26:73). That's basically the same as assuming someone is dangerous simply because they wear a hoodie at night. Or believing someone is a criminal because they are often referred to as an *"illegal alien,"* given away by their accent.

And yet on the other hand, to the Roman Empire, Galileans were unequivocally not Roman; they were Jews. They were second and third class in the Empire. And the status quo throughout the Empire made sure of it. The taxes they were charged and the inequity they faced throughout the Empire made it very clear that Jews, whether of mixed background or not, were not seen the same as pure-bred Romans.

In other words, being Galilean only widened the distance between the center of culture and the margins of culture. Being Galilean, from society's vantage point, only qualified you to be forgotten and unimportant, with no real home in society. The mother of our Lord was not unfamiliar to the tensions of living in the *remezcla*.

But maybe your *remezcla* experience isn't like mine. Perhaps it's social or circumstantial. You have several worlds colliding, but they're not necessarily ethnic worlds. Esther and Moses from the Bible are examples of this.

Both Esther and Moses found themselves enjoying life in the palace. But both were Jews, and in those times, that undoubtedly meant life in the margins, not the palace. For a part of their story, they lived trying to balance those two worlds. For Moses, the tension resulted in somewhat of an identity explosion—he murdered someone and ran into solitude for forty years in the desert. For Esther, the tension resulted in a thrust toward leadership and confidence.

But perhaps the greatest example of *remezcla* is Jesus himself. There is no other person in whom we can find two worlds crashing more powerfully and vividly. In Jesus, we find the world of heaven and the world of earth coming together. In one moment, Jesus can be pressed in by the angry crowds of his hometown, a cliff just a few feet away, but pass right through the crowds and avoid death. And yet in another moment, as a child, Jesus can feel the very real effects of a broken government whose policies displaced his family from their home. One moment Jesus can be on the top of a mountain in conversation with Moses and Elijah—men who died centuries before his birth—shining with divine and glorious and out-of-this-world radiance. And yet in another moment Jesus can sit with his friends and eat some fish. Jesus knew what it meant to be hungry, while also knowing that "man shall not live by bread alone" (Matt. 4:4 ᴇsᴠ). He knew what it meant to lose someone and weep, yet said right after the death of his friend Lazarus that "the one who believes in me, even if he dies, will live" (John 11:25).

Jesus knew what it meant to be tired. Jesus knew what it meant to work hard with his hands; to sweat like we do during a double shift at work. He also knew that his radical work on the cross would bring about eternal rest for all who would believe in his work. Jesus knew that sometimes you don't have a place to lay your head, while also promising his disciples in John 14 that he's preparing a home for us and also making it so that we are at home with him. Jesus knew how it felt to be betrayed, to know that "his own" would not receive him, yet he still died for his enemies.

Jesus knew what it meant to be here but not belong here. In him "the entire fullness of God's nature dwells" (Col. 2:9). Jesus is the *eternal* Word, wrapped in *human* flesh. Jesus wept over the city of his birth, while dying for the salvation of the world.

When it comes to the hyphenated experience (*something*-American), our cultural and ethnic roots live inside of us. That side of us desires to flourish and be cultivated. That side of us finds a lot of pride in our existence because it connects us to generations of our family. In turn, we discover more of who we are and have been created to be. On the other side of that tension, however, is our very real and strong American experience. It's in this experience that we read, think, and deliberate. Our decision-making is influenced mostly (unless we've really disciplined ourselves to think in our native tongue) by our American narrative. A side of us that has very real potential for creating, reimagining, and leaving an impact on our world in the time we have here. Both of these worlds are our own. We own both of the experiences. And we don't want either to police the other. Instead, we want both experiences to live together, to collaborate in a way that empowers us to honor both and give birth to a new social identity.

Some of this tension is hard to find language for. It often feels like all you have are your experiences. And those experiences often shape your view of the world—God, yourself, and those around you. So I've had to ask myself a lot of questions and allow my faith to shape the way I engage them.

The Fruits of the *Remezcla*

"Richa! Ven aquí!" my mom would exclaim from the kitchen. She needed me to help read and understand all the fine print of the mail that had just come in. *"Richa! Ven agárrame el teléfono!"* That was her calling me over to grab the phone from her. Probably because there was someone on the other end speaking English in a way that was intimidating to her. She was afraid that she wouldn't understand and perhaps miss or agree to something that she would later regret. This was common in my house. My siblings and I played mediator or translator all the time. But playing mediator became most real and important to me during hospital visits. I realized in those moments how important my dual reality was to my parents as they lived in a culture that only saw their shadows. I realized that my complicated, hybrid experience wasn't a curse, as my experience had often made me believe, but a blessing.

Some of the first questions I needed to wrestle with were: What can be birthed out of my *remezcla* experience? What fruits can come from these tensions?

Insight and Impact

As I've already mentioned, my life is the result of two worlds coming together "in marriage." But growing up, the marriage wasn't always perfect. In fact, oftentimes, it felt like the marriage was going to fall apart at any moment. My two worlds were often down each other's throats. Insecure of what one would do to the other. Suspicious of the kindness they communicated to one another because they seldom demonstrated it to one another. And although my two worlds came together in marriage, the reality felt more like an estranged relationship. And now here's this kid, a reminder of both . . . to both. He's got his mother's nose and his dad's temperament. He's got his mom's humor and his dad's complexion. When his dad looks at him, he reminds him too much of his mother who he wants nothing to do with. When his mom looks at him, he reminds her too much of his dad who she wants to keep her distance from. In the end, this child is a reminder to both his parents that there aren't as many barriers between them as they would like there to be.

What I've come to realize is that my experience as a Dominican-American has afforded me the blessing of insight. As a Dominican, I can understand my parents in a way that my country never could. And in possessing that knowledge I'm able to, from a safe place, a familiar place, share with my parents the ways they must grow and seize the opportunities of living in our country as best they can.

As a native-born American, immersed in American culture from a young age, I can understand my country in a way that my parents might not be able to. I'm able to, from a safe place, a familiar place (although in recent times I've come to realize that I'm not so familiar to my country), share with my country its blindspots. I can share with my country the ways in which it didn't love my "mother" the way it promised to.

Virgilio Elizondo slices right to the heart of this fruit when he says,

> The *mestizo* doesn't fit conveniently into . . . either parent group. The *mestizo* may understand them far better than they understand him or her. To be an insider-outsider, as the *mestizo*, is to have closeness to and distance from both parent cultures. A *mestizo* people can see and appreciate characteristics in its parent cultures that they can neither see in themselves nor in each other. It is threatening to be in the presence

of someone who knows us better than we know ourselves.[10]

Essentially, it seems that the *remezcla* experience empowers us to be culturally agile. We are able to live with the ability, if we learn to harness it, to navigate both worlds with significant influence, a clear vision, and a winsome posture. Perhaps this is why San Pablo (Paul) was able to declare as part of his spiel to the Corinthian church that,

> To the Jews I became like a Jew, to win Jews; to those under the law, like one under the law— though I myself am not under the law—to win those under the law. To those who are without the law, like one without the law—though I am not without God's law but under the law of Christ—to win those without the law. To the weak I became weak, in order to win the weak. I have become all things to all people, so that I may by every possible means save some. (1 Cor. 9:20–22)

Paul's dual reality, as we've already mentioned, allowed him to exist in both of his worlds in incredible ways. Acts 21–26 contain stories about Paul's journey that will leave you wondering why he didn't die a younger man. In the custody of both Jewish and Roman officials, Paul should have died at least on two occasions! Yet it was his divine placement in the intersection of Jewish, Roman, and Greek identity that empowered him to speak to all his worlds and strike conviction along the way. In one instance, Paul surprised the Roman officials when he addressed them in Greek. Then just a few moments later, he was able to hush a crowd of incited Jews by addressing them in the commonly spoken Aramaic. On two different occasions Paul is able to give witness to the incredible ways that God met him through our Lord Jesus—once to the Jews, by sharing his story as a Jew and using the law as his entry point; another time to the Roman tribune and King Agrippa himself! King Agrippa was so captured by his witness that he asked Paul in front of all who were there, "Are you going to persuade me to become a Christian so easily?" (Acts 26:28).

I wonder if this is what makes diversity or "other" so uncomfortable? Both for the one carrying the diverse experiences in themselves and also for the "parents" who gave birth to them. Perhaps this is why we might hear, "Speak English! This is America," in an effort to contain our worlds to one language, because that's easier, less complicated, and perhaps safer. Or perhaps the discomfort of diversity is the reason we try to build walls and keep the "other" experiences out in an effort to preserve what has been the comfortable and dominant culture.

There is no doubt that Paul was able to speak directly and compellingly to both his worlds. The same can be said about our *remezcla*.

Yet another question that I needed to wrestle with was: What will I need as I journey through life with my *remezcla*?

Courage

This journey, I'm realizing, demands courage to travel the "uncharted" path. Traveling off the beaten path is a little tougher, perhaps a lot tougher. Not only does it exert more physical energy, but it demands more of you mentally, emotionally, and spiritually. You often have to learn to explore the "deeps" of your mind and heart; areas of yourself you didn't know existed. Traveling off the beaten path requires you to unearth things you didn't know you had covered. Perhaps it's the reason why it's the road less traveled. But I must say, despite—and maybe because of—its difficulty, it is the most formative road. It's formative because it calls for an *honest* journey with Jesus. The kind of honesty that says, "Jesus, I believe you, but help me when I inevitably don't believe. Jesus, you are the King of creation, but help me to trust that you are the Lord of my finances . . . relationships . . . career." What I'm realizing is that this journey with Jesus demands far more than just *mere* openness, where you expose *some* of your weaknesses or even *dress up* your confessions so that ultimately you would be seen as a true model of transparency. Rather, it seems that we'll need to be fully prepared for true vulnerability, where you actually run meaningful risks. That you *may* actually lose something by being this vulnerable. It's the kind of willingness to discover that you might not fit anywhere. That you may not belong in the categories listed. That you cannot check off any of the boxes. It takes courage to keep moving ahead although there aren't many offering encouragement, and there are few spaces that understand you or are even willing to. Yet let God refresh you with the words he spoke through King David in Psalm 31:24: "Be strong, and let your heart be courageous, all you who put your hope in the Lord."

Patience

As we've already discussed, this is messy! It certainly requires thoughtfulness and patience as we navigate our complexities. As a New Yorker, this life principle is particularly challenging. We live in an area that's incredibly dense in just a one-mile radius. Packed in and stacked high. New York is often known as "the city that never sleeps," and perhaps that's because it's the city that never feels finished. It may be the reason why scaffolding feels less temporary and more like an accessory to structures around us. Everyone is always moving and always working, always trying to get more and more done. In all the moving, we're often too impatient to make room (or time, for that matter) for the most meaningful things. Far too often have we reduced the journey to and with Jesus down to linear terms—it's black or white; it's in or out; it's right or wrong. Yet very little about our experiences can be neatly categorized that way. Our lives are more nuanced than our rigid categories give room for. We will need the patience to not always have a packaged answer or resolve for our challenges and difficulties. We will need the patience to move phase by phase, step by step, one degree of understanding to another degree of understanding, one step in the direction of trust to another step deeper into trust. And maybe like Peter in Luke 5, we, too, will need the patience to see our trust of Jesus evolve into deep surrender and worship. Peter went from trusting

Jesus enough "to put out a little from the land" when Jesus asked him, to taking his boat "out into deep water and [letting] down [his] nets" (Luke 5:3–4), to finally falling to his knees and worshipping Jesus. Neatly packaged categories don't often leave room for that kind of journey. Impatience settles in when life doesn't fall into our controlled environments. We will need the patience to watch that journey of trust evolve.

Security

We will need to live with a deep sense of security. We will need it in order to know that the gospel of Jesus calls us, receives us, embraces us, understands us, loves us, transforms us, and empowers us even though we sometimes don't understand, embrace, and love ourselves. And even though others might not either.

Faith

We will need faith to believe that God has placed us here in the middle of all these intersections with a great purpose. To spearhead renewal and creativity, to call his incredibly diverse, complex, and beautiful kingdom down to earth. We will need a faith that draws strength for the journey from the greatest *remezcla* story—Jesus.

When we consider the tension-filled society we're living in, the influential and transformative figures in our world will be those who learn to be okay with tension. We must learn to listen well, and in order to do that, we must become familiar with the tension itself, either by being born into it, or by participating in it as deeply as those who've been born in it. Leaders that leave an eternal impact in our world are those who are willing to challenge, rediscover, and revitalize the norms of our world the same way Jesus did for the Jews, as much as for the Gentiles, of his world.

Ultimately, my hope is that all of us—those who do and don't live in the hyphen—will make homes and build families. My hope is that those homes and families will impact our neighborhoods. My hope is that Jesus will be made famous in all of our cities, above all things, as the Son of God who was given to us to bring us *entre familia*.

As like with the unlikely Messiah from Nazareth, love demands death. Death to self. Death to the mirage of success that society is built on, causing injustice and an abusive creation. And perhaps it demands physical death. Only God's love can break us out of our selfish layers of protection so that we can become channels of God's love even in hard places.

—Ruth Padilla DeBorst

Love makes your soul crawl out from its hiding place.

—Zora Neale Hurston

CHAPTER 3

Love Neighbor:
Quién ha Visto!

My son walked in, killin' the suit game, and strutted down the hall. He was showing us how he would walk down the aisle at our friend's wedding as the ring bearer. And then my mother-in-love (that's how I refer to her) looked at him, burst into laughter, and said, *"Pero mira este chulo! Quién ha visto!"* That's a phrase almost all Hispanics use when they see or hear something that surprises them. It's typically a good surprise, but sometimes it can be a bad one. It's also not just a simple surprise; it's something you didn't see coming at all, and it completely blows you away.

"Quién ha visto!"—Struttin'!

When we think of love, this is precisely what we should think. A love that blows us away. An expression of love that we weren't quite expecting. Frankly speaking, a love that we've never seen. Jesus' closest earthly friend, a guy named John, paints the picture for us. He wrote a letter to Jesus' followers from an island called Patmos, where he was exiled for his faith. John writes, "See what kind of love the Father has given to us, that we should be called children of God; and so we are" (1 John 3:1 ESV). What you don't hear in a simple reading of this part of God's story is the emotion it carries. After talking Jesus up for two chapters—Jesus is the greatest source of life, the greatest friend, the most faithful advocate, the brightest light—John finally explodes with emotions and asks a question about the nature of God's love for the world. You see, John wrote that letter in Greek, and the phrase *see what kind of love* is translated "of what origin, of what country."

John had never before seen, heard, or felt this kind of love. It was so foreign to him that it drove him to explode and ask, "From what country and of what origin is this love?" Like the rest of you, I'm asking, *What made this love foreign?* What drove John to explode with such emotion at the thought of this love? What was so profoundly unique about this love that he basically begged everyone to look at it and experience it?

We'll get back to this in a moment. First I want to offer some life experiences that could help us see love as John saw it.

Si tú supieras! *The Honesty of Love*

It's true that skeptics need to hear clearer arguments about our convictions and worldview. But actually— and especially when it comes to social issues—clarity is not their greatest need. In fact, for today's Christian, the best way to influence a skeptic is not through a clear argument, but through an honest and God-inspired life. By honest, I mean being emotionally and spiritually accessible. I mean being open about what keeps us from a meaningful and intimate relationship with God. By honest, I mean caring less about image and caring more about identity.

I read short stories and memoirs far more often than I write them. But from time to time—or *de temps en temps,* as my wife likes to say (she's a French enthusiast)—I enjoy grabbing certain life experiences, turning them into short stories, and publishing them anywhere I can. I figure that one day my kids will get hold of them, read them, and find them a source of joy. I really enjoyed writing this one story called "Home Base." I posted it on Instagram with a photograph to help the reader better enter into the story. "Home Base" was a hit! A ton of people enjoyed it and shared it through social media. The story captures the relationship between a dad and his son, and highlights the son's longing for his dad's attention, affection, and approval. All his life is a performance in which he seeks those things from his father. The story ends with a string of questions intended to stir up readers and help them realize that the relationship between father and son is best hinged on identity rather than on performance. There is nothing the son can do, nor anything he can perform, that will earn or lose his father's affection. The son's home base, so to speak, is not what he can do—but, rather, who he is.

Of all the reactions to the story, the one that most captured my attention was from an old high school classmate. He isn't particularly sympathetic toward Christianity; in fact, he very confidently considers himself an atheist. Needless to say, our conversations are always interesting. His response was simple but also very encouraging, because I felt it was an indicator of what we all long for essentially. He said, "This [post] hit me unlike other posts do. Salute." He went on to share that, as a soon-to-be father, he had been thinking about what that relationship was going to look like for his family. My story would help him think a little more deeply about relationships, fatherhood, sacrifice, and love. I was so grateful for his honesty. I was grateful that my story was able to strike that chord and get him thinking.

As a Christian, my desire is that my relationships lead to friends knowing Jesus. Only then can friends become true family. I'm realizing that it is important that our lives as Christians have that kind of effect on the people around us.

I remember when my wife and I led a premarital counseling session with a couple of our friends. The soon-to-be-bride said she felt like she had no one to talk to about the conflicts that she and her fiancé were experiencing. I asked why, and she responded that many of the married people around her didn't show signs of conflict, or at least of any deep conflict. If they had conflicts, they did a good job of masking them. All of this, she concluded, contributed to her and her fiancé confronting their obstacles poorly, and thus jeopardizing the health of their relationship and future marriage.

My heart broke for them. I realized that failing to live honestly is failing to live with faithful influence, and that living honestly—as I described honesty earlier—makes us accessible. Because the experiences in marriage and relationship of most families in her life were not accessible to her, our friend couldn't gain insight and wisdom from them.

In Matthew 22:37–40, Jesus makes it plain: "Love the Lord your God with all your heart, with all your soul, and with all your mind. This is the greatest and most important command. The second is like it: Love your neighbor as yourself. All the Law and the Prophets depend on these two commands."

In essence, Jesus takes all the stories of the Bible—all the historical accounts, the poetry, the prophecy, and the wisdom literature—and condenses their message down to a tweet. And Jesus' several million followers probably would generate several hundred thousand retweets, shares, and comments on that post. But although I think that our generation has leveraged social media effectively in the face of great social turmoil, and that we've seen several heroes emerge from it, we are still largely a generation with merely social media activists. One hundred and forty characters is not remotely equivalent to 140 hours of personal, intimate time with people, working for causes and for truth. The problem is that intimacy demands openness, and quite frankly, some of us are far too afraid to be *that* honest. It's hard work! How many of us would not only retweet this "love God, love others" tweet by Jesus, but would commit ourselves to the hard work of living it?

Ponte claro! *The Sincerity of Love*

A good friend of mine has been known to say that "authenticity is our generation's apologetic." At home, we would just say, *"Ponte claro, manito!"* In other words, "Get clear! Quick!" For the Christian today, the greatest form of influence is an honest life. Who would've thought, right? Who would have thought that building strong relationships requires being vulnerable and acknowledging our weaknesses and inadequacies—but even more, that our brokenness would be so valuable? Who would've thought that leaving space for other people to experience those dark things about you creates space in which Jesus can be the hero? But what does being honest look like? What does it take to love our neighbors well?

There is *una historia*—a folktale, if you would—in Roman and Greek history about dishonest sculptors in

the marketplace. These are the salesmen who are concerned primarily with making a profit, even if it means
they have to be creepy, weird, and persistent about getting customers to buy their product rather than anyone
else's. (For the New Yorker, think of Canal Street.
I know I do.) At any rate, these sculptors take their
imperfect sculptures, patch the holes and cracks with
wax, and tag them as their best and most perfect items.
(Again, I think about my countless "Iceberg" sweaters
and "Tag Heuer" watches. But whatever. I'm not bitter.) Market-goers buy these "perfect" items, believing
themselves fortunate to come away with such bargains.
But when a shrewd customer walks by, the dishonest
sellers don't stand a chance. Shrewd customers know
to simply hold the "perfect" items up to the light of the
sun, and then they can quickly spot the imperfections.
Like any of us would do, the customers demand their
money back and also ask the sellers to stop deceptively
marking these imperfect sculptures—and their holes
covered with wax—as "perfect."

Sometimes it feels like we love people the same way
these guys sell their merchandise—dishonestly. Our
relationships are covered in wax. We are covered in
wax. We don't allow anyone to see our imperfections.

We present ourselves as perfect items, and in doing so, we discourage real relationships from forming.

I love the way Rebecca Pippert puts it. She says, "One thing that's hurting the church is the heresy of niceness. We give the impression that now that we're Christians, we swing from one victory to the next. But that's not real and it won't attract real people. We have the power to overcome our sins, but we cannot overcome what we refuse to admit. That's the tension we must live in. It has to be authentic."[1]

Tucked away in one of the most colossal letters of the Bible is this little verse: "Love must be sincere" (Rom. 12:9 NIV). For my Spanish speakers, that word *sincere* might sound familiar. The word comes from the Latin *sin cera*, literally translated as "without wax." Simply put, the way to love someone well is to share your life with them, the bad as much as the good. The things worth challenging as much as the things worth celebrating. Love without wax.

Sin vergüenza! *The Hospitality of Love*

When we talk about living with that level of authenticity, one of the few places you're sure to see it lived out is at home. Growing up and even today, it's at home and in most of my relatives' homes that we frequently call each other *"sin vergüenza!"* It literally means "of no shame," but it wasn't used entirely that way. It's used as if to say, "Don't you dare ask me for anything while you're here! This is your house too! And I don't want you to feel anything other than that!" The exclamation points are appropriate. It always felt as though they were yelling at me. I didn't know if I should be offended and tell my parents to stand up for me or not. But of course, it was a warm welcome into the environment and not an insult at all.

Your home is one of the most intimate spaces in your life, no matter what it looks like. It's where you retreat from the craziness of life, or it's the place that you want no one to know about because the brokenness in it is overwhelming and you'd rather keep home—well . . . at home. Whatever your home looks like, it is certainly one of the spaces of your life with major influence—positive or negative. So what would it look like to open the doors to our lives a bit more than we normally do? *Sheesh!* Nerve-racking. But what if we had a different understanding of hospitality? What if maximizing our lives is done best by investing them in someone other than ourselves? What if gaining is best experienced by giving? What would it look like to slowly invite people into our mess? How would it challenge us? Change us? How would it inspire our environment?

Interestingly enough, the idea of hospitality seems to be a common thing in our culture. In other words, it's common to invite people over to eat a meal, or for a game night. It's common to welcome people to enjoy a get-together. In fact, various cultures are built around the concept of hospitality. But there are a few tensions we try to consider in the Pérez home.

No Room for Your Hospitality

For one thing, hospitality cannot be narrowly defined. In places like New York—where we're packed in and stacked high, and where the kitchen and living room in an apartment might be one small, combined space—inviting people over for the sake of hospitality might be common, but it also can be really overwhelming, even for extroverts! Hospitality has to go far beyond just opening the doors to your home, because in New York, some homes barely have a door. If we define hospitality narrowly, then there are very few people who can faithfully live it out. So here's how we define it: hospitality means extending to other people the things in your life that refresh you most.

People Are the Priority

The second tension we consider is the "who" of hospitality. The question isn't, "Are we showing hospitality?" The question is, "To whom are we showing hospitality?" When it comes to true hospitality, as God tells the story, people are the priority. We should show hospitality to one another, as sisters and brothers in the faith community. God calls us to share with one another generously and to welcome other people into our lives. Hospitality deepens Christian community and strengthens Christian witness.

Yet our hospitality should reach far beyond our faith community. Let's consider what God means when he reminds us to "seek to show hospitality" (Rom. 12:13 ESV). The English language has a way of not fully capturing the meat, so to speak, of the words in God's story, which were originally written in Greek and Hebrew. The word *hospitality* is made up of two Greek words. The first is *philo*, which means "deep sibling-like love." It's why Philadelphia is called the city of brotherly love. The second Greek word is *xeno*, which means "stranger." That's where we get the word *xenophobia*, the fear of strangers. When God is thinking of hospitality, the first person he has in mind is not our friend or people with whom we are familiar. He's thinking of the stranger, the person with whom we are not familiar.

But it gets even more challenging. The word *xeno* also means "immigrant," the foreigner among us—the person who doesn't speak the dominant language, who's treated as a second-class person, and who's often left on the margins. And it gets worse! These words in Greek and Hebrew are so beefy that we need a whole family of words in English to capture their meaning. In ancient Israel, because immigrants and foreigners were often enemies also, *xeno* also evolved to mean "enemy."

Now the concept of hospitality doesn't just mean inviting friends over for dinner; rather, it's about loving strangers and enemies in the same way we love siblings.

Refreshment Is the Purpose

There's a little story tucked away in the Old Testament, in which we see a valuable principle lived out. In 2 Kings 4:8–37, we read the story of one of God's prophets and a woman from a city called Shunem. The Shunammite woman notices that on his way to a place called Carmel, Elisha, God's prophet, always passes by her family's way. She thinks to herself, *I'm wealthy and prominent, plus I'm sure he could use a rest stop between*

Carmel and wherever he's traveling from. Let's build a room on our roof and offer him that space to relax, read, pray, eat, and sleep. So she does just that.

Elisha is blown away by her hospitality and her willingness to offer to him the things that bring her refreshment—home, family, and food. So Elisha looks at his servant and says, "Yo! Call that woman over." Then in verse 13 he says, "You've gone to all this trouble for us. What can we do for you? Can we speak on your behalf to the king or to the commander of the army?" The Shunammite woman answered, "I am living among my own people."

What this women means is that the best place for hospitality to grow is not from deep-rooted obligation, but rather from deep-rooted intimacy and contentment with God and his people. In other words, those of us practicing hospitality with a greater level of effect and influence are those of us enjoying God and the faith community deeply and often.

When it comes to true hospitality, the church exists to display the goodness and peace of God in Jesus by making family out of strangers, friends out of enemies, and homes out of brokenness. Just like this Shunammite woman with Elisha, hospitality makes refreshment its purpose. Hospitality says, "I cannot have you come around me without feeling a deep desire to bring you the things that give me refreshment."

Arroz Con Habichuelas *at the Table*

Over the years I've seen the value of hospitality as a way to love neighbors well. I once had a young man, maybe seventeen years old, say to me after visiting one of our church services, "Hey, I don't have much money to give to the church, but maybe you can come play some Play Station in my room sometime." He continued, "I'd love to have you and your family over." I was completely taken aback. On one hand, I got it. Kids from this neighborhood are starved for older male role models and mentors. On the other hand, that kind of private space is typically closed off to people with whom you don't have a long-standing relationship. I was shocked—but at the same time pleasantly welcomed, not into a space, but into someone's life.

I'll never forget the expression on a good friend's face the first time I invited him to dinner with my family. He was a young high school student whom I had been mentoring through a local program. We had been hanging out only for about a month before I extended the invitation. He came over, ate *arroz con habichuelas,* sat through my son's burps at the table, and wasn't fazed by his very seven-year-old, imaginative conversations. He joined us in prayer, enjoyed my thirty-one-year-old jokes, and was very sweet with my daughter and wife. I could tell that he was trying to wrap his mind around being not simply in our apartment, in our home, but that he also was somehow refreshingly disarmed by it. During dinner at our home, he realized that his pastor-friend-mentor was just a typical guy with flaws, who laughed and drank *morir soñando* just like most Dominicans Uptown. He was able to see how I treat women, such as my wife and daughter, and—more important—why I treat them that way. He also was able to see what pushes my buttons, what tests my patience, and how I, like anyone else, sometimes had to ask for forgiveness. At home, I wasn't able to hide.

It's really incredible, when you come to see the heart of God's story. Dead center in God's story is unimaginable hospitality. Take the opening scene of the Bible, for example. God, who has existed throughout eternity, creates the heavens and the earth. In the middle of his creation is a garden. And then toward the end of the first chapter of Genesis, we see this happen:

Then God said, "Let us make man in our image, according to our likeness." . . . And God said to them, "Be fruitful, multiply, and fill the earth and subdue it. Rule the fish of the sea, the birds of the skies, and every creature that crawls on the earth." God also said, "Look, I have given you every seed-bearing plant on the surface of the entire earth and every tree whose fruit contains seed. This will be food for you." (Gen. 1:26–29)

God creates a space and invites us into it. He says to Adam and Eve, "Come in, use the space as your own, bring your family into the space, and enjoy whatever the space offers you." God's kindness, generosity, and love make room for Adam and Eve to know him intimately and enjoy the world he has created for all of them.

Or what about Deuteronomy 10? In this story is a reminder to Israel that they need to be unique, distinct from the nations around them. One of their distinctions would be authenticity and commitment to God, which would produce great love and compassion. God is described as the God who "executes justice for the fatherless and the widow, and loves the sojourner, giving him food and clothing" (v. 18 ESV). Then God calls Israel to "Love the sojourner, therefore, for [they] were sojourners in the land of Egypt" (v. 19 ESV). Again, here's another reminder that God's intentions have always been to welcome the foreigner into an environment where they would be refreshed. Think of the effect this particular portion of God's story would have if we took it to heart. Think of the profound and lasting influence this would have on the majority of kids around our country, particularly in inner cities, if we allowed ourselves to be inspired by God's version of hospitality. Think of the single-parent homes and the elderly, the widowed neighbors and coworkers. Think of the mother who works tirelessly for her kids to piece things together after her husband has left her alone. Think of the emotional energy required just to endure life in our beloved American cities, let alone to thrive in them. What does it mean to "execute justice for the fatherless and the widow"? What does it mean to offer them "food and clothing"—the things they need most? Although we might have different ideas about what this means, we can all agree that it at least means to invite people to share in the things that refresh us.

Or consider King David in 2 Samuel 9:1–13. Years after the death of Saul, one of his greatest enemies, David asks his closest officials an unbelievable question: "Is there anyone remaining from the family of Saul I can show kindness to for Jonathan's sake?" (v. 1). He wants to show kindness to his enemy's family? After all the headaches (a gross understatement) he caused for David's family? As time passed, David learned that there was, in fact, a grandson of Saul, the only person left from his family lineage. His name was Mephibosheth, and David relentlessly pursued him until he finally found him. Then David made a promise to him. "So Mephibosheth ate at David's table just like one of the king's sons" (v. 11). Rather than wiping Saul's heritage off the face of the earth, he extended unimaginable hospitality to the last member of Saul's family and welcomed Mephibosheth as one of his own. Verse 13 ends that story: "However, Mephibosheth lived in Jerusalem because he always ate at the king's table."

But perhaps the oddest detail to this episode between David and Mephibosheth is the last verse—verse 13. It describes Mephibosheth as "lame in both his feet" (ESV). In other words, he's unable to walk on his own! It doesn't take much to imagine the work and intentionality it requires to meet the needs of someone who doesn't have the privilege of being able to pick up and go whenever they want or even as quickly as they want. Most of us have been around or responsible for someone with physical disabilities. In public buses, school buses, in building entrances and several other spaces—it takes just a little longer for something to get done or started or moved along. Let's be frank: our culture sees the disabled as an inconvenience. Perhaps even as second class. They don't have the privilege of moving as quickly as others do and if they can't move quickly they'll always fall behind in the race for a better job with the higher salary. Again, if it slows me down, if it hampers my time line or plan, it's inconvenient. Seldom do we stop to think of how we may use our privilege of walking to the benefit of those who can't. This story between David and Mephibosheth shows us that hospitality may be inconvenient sometimes, but it is in the very nature of hospitality to leverage what is a benefit and privilege to you for the benefit of others.

Man! Thinking through just these few examples raises several questions about loving our cities well. For instance, I wonder how this vision of hospitality would inform the way we see the immigrant community in our neighborhoods. I wonder what this vision of hospitality means for the 3,100 homeless students in our community alone. I often think of the people in my own life who have left a significant imprint. The men and women who permanently etched their influence in my life were people who shared time with me, not merely words. The people who become indispensable in my life are the people who, to this day, still have a voice in my life.

When I was growing up, my all-time favorite TV show was *The Fresh Prince of Bel-Air*, starring my favorite actor, Will Smith. The sitcom was filled with all sorts of funny and memorable moments, but none more memorable than in season four with Will and his father, Lou. If you're a fan, you know this episode very well. It seemed like one of the most—if not the most—defining moments of the show. In an effort to mend the hurts he caused Will by abandoning him fourteen years earlier, Lou invites his son to go on the road with him. But then he has a cowardly moment and tries to sneak off and leave Will behind. Will, oblivious to everything, comes out ready to hit the road with his dad. And just as he did fourteen years earlier, Lou disappoints Will again by rambling on with an excuse about having to switch up the plans. Extremely disappointed, Will runs down every reason he doesn't need a father. "He wasn't there to teach me how to shoot my first basket," he said. "I got through my first date without him, I learned how to drive without him, I learned how to shave, I learned how to fight without him!" Unable to mask his hurt anymore,

Will breaks down. Through his tears, he asks Uncle Phil a question: "How come he don't want me, man?"[2]

At that moment, Phil—Will's uncle by marriage—doesn't say much, and he doesn't try to offer a solution. He simply embraces Will. In fact, throughout the whole scene, Uncle Phil is just there—listening, affirming, comforting. And finally, embracing. As you watch, you realize that Will just wanted someone—anyone—to invite him in, understand him, guide him, and love him. Will wanted the refreshment of a real relationship. Instead, he was once again left out to dry. But guess who was there to offer comfort. It was Uncle Phil who knew that Will's jump shot had gotten better. But how did he know? Because he was at Will's games. It was Uncle Phil who knew that Will had learned how to shave. How did he know? Because it was in his bathroom that Will learned it. It was Uncle Phil who knew about Will's love life, because he let Will borrow his car for dates and offered him advice. Uncle Phil did not merely open the doors of his house to Will—he opened the doors of his life.

Hospitality is at the heart of the story of God. Consider the life of Jesus. At the cross, Jesus makes possible again what had been ours in the beginning—a relationship with God in the home he created for all of us. In fact, I've heard it said that all of life is a journey back to the garden. Certainly in John 14:1–3 Jesus captures this perfectly. After preparing his closest friends to hear some of the most difficult news they'll ever hear, Jesus says to them, "Don't let your heart be troubled. Believe in God; believe also in me. In my Father's house are many rooms; if not, I would have told you. I am going away to prepare a place for you. If I go away and prepare a place for you, I will come again and take you to myself, so that where I am you may be also."

What is incredibly profound about this is not that Jesus suddenly becomes Bob the Builder in heaven, fixing us up a dope spot, but rather that he defines our ultimate place of home and rest wherever he is. In other words, Jesus says that although eternity in heaven is going be amazing, real eternal bliss is wherever his presence is found. We spend our lives trying to fit in, trying to find love and acceptance—from everyone except the one true source, Jesus. Jesus is the person and place where we can feel safest to be ourselves—loose screws and all—and find forgiveness, clarity, refreshment, and new life.

That's comforting, because life is tough and it hurts most of the time. It's comforting because we don't often find our place. It's comforting because some of us don't feel welcomed anywhere. It's comforting because some of us live in depression, abandonment, and loneliness, and home seems to us like a nebulous thought. It's comforting because now home isn't a place, but a person. It's comforting because home has a name: Jesus.

The Wonder of Love

Do you remember Jesus' friend John? You remember him exploding with emotion, calling us to "see what great love the Father has given us" (1 John 3:1)? It's no surprise that John, doing his best to help us "see what great love," is the same John who sat at the foot of the cross while Jesus barely got his last words out.

Imagine with me what happened during those moments. Jesus is hanging on a cross, and with every passing moment, he gradually loses the ability to breathe, making every single breath and word precious. He can barely see, because he's losing oxygen and blood is dripping over his eyes. But somehow he looks out to the crowd and sees his closest friend, John, and Mary, his mother. John sees the agony his friend is unjustly forced to endure, and then Jesus does the unthinkable. He musters up whatever oxygen and energy he has left, and he says these last and bloody words: "Father, forgive them, for they know not what they do" (Luke 23:34 ESV).

Considering this, there's no doubt that John would urge us to "see what kind of love the Father has given to us." In just ten words, Jesus teaches us more about being brave than anything else will ever teach us. In ten words, he shows us what's at the heart of his story. In ten words, Jesus gives us the secret to dealing with hurt. In ten words, Jesus shows us the way to healthy relationships. And in ten words, Jesus champions the way to love our neighbor.

When my wife and I got married, we both came into the relationship with relational baggage, just like . . . well, everyone. It proved difficult to shed that baggage. Our past relationships had left wounds, which we brought into our marriage. I particularly remember saying to her, "Hey, I've never hurt you this way. Why does it seem like I'm paying for what another guy did? Why am I picking up someone else's mess?"

Then *bang!* God's words hit me: "Each one of us is to please his neighbor for his good, to build him up. For even Christ did not please himself. On the contrary, as it is written, The insults of those who insulted you have fallen on me" (Rom. 15:2–4), and, "Carry one another's burdens; in this way you will fulfill the law of Christ" (Gal. 6:2).

I realized that if we want to know Jesus' love for the world, if we want to experience his love, our concern shouldn't be to impress anyone. Our concern should be the burdens of others, the broken pieces around us, the mess in our relationships—especially the ones we didn't cause.

What drove John to his emotional explosion was this: at the heart of Jesus' love is a relentless pursuit of his bride, untethered to anyone's impression or response. Loving your neighbor means picking up the pieces of their brokenness. Loving your neighbor means helping to clean up someone else's mess. Loving your neighbor means becoming a servant with nothing to prove and everyone to serve!

When that thought seems overwhelming, I've always drawn strength and inspiration in the way Justo González puts it:

> You don't wait for others to live by this philosophy of love in order to live by it yourself. It is precisely because others don't live by a vision of love that you will often pay for it. You unmask the evils of society by taking it upon yourself. This is what happened with MLK Jr.; this is what happened with Cesar Chavez; and that is what happened with Jesus at the cross.[3]

Y decirle al Señor este es mi plan. Si es tu voluntad, lleva este plan acabo // And tell the Lord "this is my plan." If it be your will, bring this plan to life.

—Carmen Amparo Pérez

Because He came into the world and into history, because He broke the silence and the agony, because He filled the earth with His glory, because He was light in our cold night. . . .

Therefore we have hope today, Therefore we fight on tenaciously today, Therefore today we look confidently on the future of this land of mine.

—Federico Jose Paruga

CHAPTER 4

Trust Jesus, Die Well:
Todo Tiene Su Final

I must have been driving at least sixty miles per hour across the George Washington Bridge after hearing the news, and my thoughts were probably racing as fast as the car. Anna sat next to me, tense and not wanting to utter a word or even look in my direction because I was so upset. We finally reached the hospital, and I left my car running out front for the valet to worry about. Columbia Presbyterian Hospital is always crowded. The hospital sits right on Broadway, and it's the one major hospital in the neighborhood, making it one of the few spots where people west of Broadway and people east of the avenue find themselves in the same place. It was incredibly difficult getting past security, but Anna and I finally got through and hurried to the elevator, which slowly and turbulently made its way to the sixth floor. With every floor we passed, I was tortured by a *beep* that reminded me of the machine to which my mother was strapped in her ICU room.

The doors slid open slowly, and we were met by a group of at least fifteen family and friends. Although it was comforting to know my mother had many supporters, I wasn't very encouraged by that sight. In my mind, it meant that she wasn't doing very well and that everyone was there to brace themselves for the worst. Over the next several hours, the crowd doubled in size and invaded the waiting room. Some people were clustered in smaller groups praying. Others sat in different corners of the room, weeping or sleeping, exhausted from worry and pacing. I remember being crouched next to a big blue bin into which the nurses flung those old, white linens with the thin blue lines around the edges. It's an odd detail, but I remember wanting to grab one of the linens to hide my tear-washed face.

Finally, I had endured enough of the doctors not letting us into her room to see her and learn her condition. I ran past a few nurses and through the automatic doors that led right to the ICU units. My mom's room was the first room to the left, and the doors were wide open. Then I saw something that'll be etched in my mind forever—a group of four or five doctors and a handful of nurses trying to keep my mother alive. There was a lot of scurrying, talking, ordering, and instructing. "Pass me the . . . !" "One, two, . . . !" "Do it now, doctor!" "Come on!" On one of their attempts to revive her with the defibrillator, my mom's body lunged up about a foot off the bed. I froze. I didn't know what to think. I didn't know what to do. My eyes, I imagine, were as wide as the windows in that room, letting in the bright August afternoon sun. One of the nurses noticed me and walked over. "You probably shouldn't be here," she said, and walked me back to the waiting room.

About ten minutes later, a doctor quietly and respectfully slid into our prayer circle. He didn't join in prayer—he simply stood there with his head down, probably thinking how to share the news. I like to think that he was asking God for the right words, because he cared about the patient's family enough to gently steward the moments that would follow. When he sensed a lull in the prayer, he shared the two most earth-shattering words I had ever heard: "She passed." I couldn't believe my ears. Those two words reverberated in me as loudly and profoundly as if I had been standing next to the Catholic church bell tower at midnight. Nothing has ever challenged my faith in Jesus more than those two simple words.

The Taste of Victory—*El Sabor de Victoria*

Everything after that was a blur. It seemed as if time stopped and everyone moved in slow motion. My dad fell to the ground in tears, with my mother's best friend trying to embrace him as he fell. My wife just looked at me, but I didn't shed even one tear. My mother's death wasn't real to me in that moment.

It took some time for me to come to grips with her passing. My mourning, a season that will never really end entirely, was initially very difficult. And even today, thinking of my mother can sometimes be difficult. It's not that thinking about her always makes me sad, or that I try to avoid the harsh realities of my life. Not at all. My faith in Jesus has helped me develop a healthy approach to loss, but it has also been the only reason that my loss hasn't crushed me. Life is beautiful, and yet also dark and difficult. Seasons of mourning remind me that in this life, *todo tiene su final*, as my friend Tony has printed on one of his T-shirts. Everything in this life has an expiration date. Yet I'll never forget the words my mother shared with me behind a curtain in the emergency room on August 7, the night before she died. A gang of family members were angry because I took way too long in the room with her, but the security guard wouldn't let anyone else pass because it was one visitor at a time. Mami and I told jokes, talked about Anna, and just didn't rush. As our laughter died down, she took the opportunity to share something. She said, "*Mijo, sé que es difícil verme de esta manera. A pesar de que este cáncer me está robando el gozo de ver a mis nietos, a pesar de que esta enfermedad me está robando la dicha de pasar más años con tu padre y aunque me está robando la alegría de ver cómo resulta la vida de tu hermano menor, a pesar de que esta situación se siente como una pérdida, este cáncer no me ha quitado el sabor de la victoria en Jesús.*"

Simply put, she said, "Although all this seems dark, I can taste victory all the more."

Enjoying a last laugh with my mom at my wedding.

I couldn't imagine what she meant by *tasting the victory of Jesus* while she sat in a hospital room suffering from cancer. Her optimism made me incredibly upset. But far beyond how I felt at that moment, she was teaching me a profoundly transcendent lesson. What I couldn't understand at that time, as mature as I thought I was in my Christian faith, was that spiritual maturity isn't measured by how much of life you've rationalized or categorized. My mom—like many mothers and fathers, *abuelas* and *abuelos*, and *tíos* and *tías* in the Hispanic heritage—didn't intellectualize her faith in Jesus. She had personal, consequential faith. She operated from a simple, almost intrinsic trust and love in the God whom she believed held her life in his hands. My mom, in that moment, was teaching me about leading a life that trusts Jesus, no questions asked. In that moment my mother put my knowledge of Jesus to shame. "*Mijo*, trust isn't neatly packaged," she said. "It's lived out in the messiness and, quite often, the difficulties of life." I couldn't see it then, but Mami had given me a real-life picture of what God communicates to us through Jeremiah:

> The person who trusts in the LORD, whose confidence indeed is the LORD, is blessed. He will

be like a tree planted by water: it sends its roots out toward a stream, it doesn't fear when heat comes, and its foliage remains green. It will not worry in a year of drought or cease producing fruit. (Jer. 17:7–8)

Crouching over in an ER unit that night gave me what classroom lectures never could—namely, a faith and trust that went beyond arguments or propositions. In those very moments between my mother, myself, and Jesus, I felt a deep sense of trust and legacy growing in me. In those moments, I was offered a picture of what my life, too, could look like in the darkest moments with which I would inevitably be confronted. In those moments, I realized that what I believed would be pushed and tested, ultimately proving whether or not trust had truly seeped into the fabric of who I was.

Two Questions

Life moved on. And so, I had to also. But that episode in my life didn't drift into the past without marking my present in some significant way. In my time of mourning and grieving, God often brought to memory another mother-son relationship that the Bible tells us about—Eunice and her son Timothy. Timothy would become like a son to Paul as they traveled most of the known world, sharing the news of Jesus and starting churches. At one point in their journey, Paul said to Timothy, "I recall your sincere faith that first lived in your grandmother Lois and in your mother Eunice and now, I am convinced, is in you also" (2 Tim. 1:5).

In the months and years that followed *Mami's* death, Scriptures like the ones above were life giving. They served as a reminder that her life would be best honored not by simple flowers at her gravesite—those were often washed away by rain before the next time I would visit. Instead, what best honors her life and faith is my own fight to trust Jesus and die as well as she did. I don't mean to sound morbid, but I am learning that as a Christian, there is a sense in which life is, in some ways, about learning to die well.

Everyone—no matter your heritage, culture, status, or circumstance—will ultimately have to answer two questions: *What is life?* and *What is death?* Or perhaps in more practical terms, what is of utmost importance and value to you, and what is the greatest opponent to that which you value most?

Although it wasn't entirely easy for my mother to come to grips with the likelihood of her leaving behind family, she very convincingly embraced the thought of her *falling asleep,* as the Bible often describes it when Christians passed away. But if I'm honest, in that conversation with my mother, I grew more and more upset because it seemed as though she was answering those two life questions and I wasn't happy with her answers. It became absolutely clear that her answer in the face of death echoed the answer of Paul as he faced death himself. "For me, to live is Christ and to die is gain" (Phil. 1:21).

Being a few years into my spiritual journey with Jesus, I knew this was the right answer. Yet in another sense I didn't know this as the answer. In those precious moments with my mother I realized that for me to live was *family* and to die was *loss.* For me, to live was *closeness* and to die was *separation.* For me, to live was *comfort* and to die was *difficulty.* For me, to live was *security* and to die was *uncertainty.*

The Disinterested Giant

Despite the reality that she was on the verge of losing something so unbelievably precious to her, death was not stripping my mother of her most valued treasure. In her case, and in the case of countless believers in Jesus, death was not an opponent, but an unintentional advocate. For the Christian, life is summed up not by achievements and accolades, but by the transcendent work and gift of Jesus. Although death in this life is never easy (it's taken me years to confidently walk in the truths I'm sharing), the news of Jesus coming to undo the brokenness of our lives and our world saps death of its most powerful weapon: separation from the presence of God himself.

Most of us walk through life with a sense of how we answer those two questions (What is life? What is death?). While all of us may use different language to answer those questions, it seems to me that in the end, we all have a form of the same sentiment: for me to live is self and to die is loss. It's difficult to not think of life in terms of your own wins, in terms of what benefits you. Our tendency is to make ourselves the biggest, central thing in our world. That might sound normal and perhaps some of us may not see anything dangerously wrong with it. Yet woven into that same strand of thinking, I believe, is deception.

G. K. Chesterton tells a parable of a young boy who once had the opportunity to become big or small. As expected, the boy chose to become a giant. The parable goes on to describe how the boy, now giant, would kick Mount Everest around like a sandcastle and would jog across the North American continent in just three minutes. Yet as exciting as this sounded, the young boy grew disinterested very quickly as the world was very small to him. Just as it was for this young boy, our tendency is to build the world around ourselves. Our natural inclination is to make ourselves the biggest narrative. And the truth is that while that may seem normal, it is dangerously misleading. Just as it was for this young boy, when we make ourselves the center of our world, we rob ourselves of the greatest joy: the joy of knowing that life, although it involves us, is much more than us. The preservation of self robs us from the joy of knowing Jesus at all. When for us *to live is self*, then certainly *to die is anything that calls you to think, and live, outside of yourself.*

In his sinless life, unjust death, and world-altering resurrection, Jesus offers what most of us live our lives uncertain about: life beyond death. The life and work of Jesus confronts any and all of the things we fear in this life, while at the same time offering us the comfort of knowing that what we know in this life—the uncertainty, the pain, the difficulty, the betrayal, the injustice, the poverty, the humiliation—isn't all that we *will* know. In the moment of greatest darkness, greatest hurt, and greatest difficulty, my mother was certain of something far greater than what the circumstance was offering her. She was certain of Jesus' victory over death. She could, in fact, taste it.

Trust Jesus that the story he's written offers a comfort far beyond whatever comfort anything in this world can offer. Trust Jesus that the story he's written offers a security far beyond whatever security anything in this world can offer. Trust Jesus that the story he's written offers a longing for approval that goes far beyond whatever longing for approval anything in this world can offer. Trust Jesus and the news of his death and resurrection enough to say with confidence, even in the darkest moments, "For me, to live is Christ and to die is gain."

How you define life will determine how you define death. The moment you determine the essence of why you're alive is the moment you determine your greatest obstacle. Once God got a hold of me and I finally discovered Jesus as my life, death no longer meant loss. I was free to invest without fear of loss, give without fear of betrayal, and love without fear of hurt. Our cities are desperate for this reality. Our generation is desperate for this sort of engagement. As I learned from Carmen Pérez, when Christ becomes my life, I'm not only free, but I'm empowered to pour myself out in the service of others. I'm able to live my life with legacy in mind.

The gospel of Jesus is my one tool to plant myself in a community for decades with hopes to see justice and godly fruit—and yet not be controlled by the fear that my life will have been in vain. The gospel of Jesus is the only truth that empowers me to make New York City my coffin and God my glory. The gospel of Jesus is the only truth that embeds me in the renewal of this city so deeply that I would say with Walt Whitman just a few months before his death in 1892, "If you want me again, look for me under your boot soles." He had given so much of himself to the love and care of the city of New York that generations after him could get a sense of his commitment from the ground of the very city he served.

I love my city and I love my neighborhood, but sometimes I worry about what it may become. Whose story will be forgotten? Whose experience will become extinct? As a resident here, I do what I can to tell the story and build the culture. As a spiritual leader here, I teach, inspire, and lead a movement that shares the truths of Jesus and confronts evil. In the end, I don't know what our efforts will produce. Yet I am certain that all of us are here to believe, work toward, expect, hope, and pray that the kingdom of God draws just a bit closer because of our lives by faith in Christ.

Perhaps, those of us living and serving in our historical moment can find comfort in words like the ones Joel shared with Israel:

> Even now—this is the LORD's declaration—turn to me with all your heart, with fasting, weeping, and mourning. Tear your hearts, not just your clothes, and return to the LORD your God. For he is gracious and compassionate, slow to anger, abounding in faithful love, and he relents from sending disaster. Who knows? He may turn and relent and leave a blessing behind him. (Joel 2:12–14)

Café En El Campo

It's been said that just before he shared his famous "I Have a Dream" speech in the presence of millions on August 28, 1963, MLK Jr. was meditating on Zechariah 8:2–8.

> This is what the LORD Almighty says: "I am very jealous for Zion; I am burning with jealousy for her."
>
> This is what the LORD says: "I will return to Zion and dwell in Jerusalem. Then Jerusalem

will be called the Faithful City, and the mountain of the LORD Almighty will be called the Holy Mountain."

This is what the LORD Almighty says: "Once again men and women of ripe old age will sit in the streets of Jerusalem, each of them with cane in hand because of their age. The city streets will be filled with boys and girls playing there."

This is what the LORD Almighty says: "It may seem marvelous to the remnant of this people at that time, but will it seem marvelous to me?" declares the LORD Almighty.

This is what the LORD Almighty says: "I will save my people from the countries of the east and the west. I will bring them back to live in Jerusalem; they will be my people, and I will be faithful and righteous to them as their God." (NIV)

I believe it. The similarities are there. And while some may see it as a naive vision, perhaps a far-fetched vision, it's inspiring nonetheless. It's inspiring because despite adverse circumstances, all is not lost. Jesus made sure that death, injustice, darkness, and evil would not have the last say on what our cities look like. Instead, he bore the weight of injustice, darkness, brokenness, and, ultimately, death. He made it possible for us to dream and work toward that faithful and fruitful city where we will be his people and he will be our God.

Juan Luis Guerra, a Dominican singer and songwriter, describes a place similar to Zechariah and MLK Jr.—the kind of place we're all hoping for—in his famous song, *"Ojalá Que Llueva Café."* He vividly describes a place where the rain pouring down from the sky is coffee, yucca, and tea. A place where instead of leaves falling from trees it would be sweet potatoes and strawberries in the fall. A place where the hills are made of brown rice. A place where instead of dew, the morning would offer a mist of white cheese. It's all very vivid and playful imagery, but it all comes together in his last few lines:

> Pa' que en este mundo no se sufra tanto
> ojalá que llueva café en el campo
> Pa' que todos los niños canten este canto
> ojalá que llueva café en el campo
> ojalá que llueva, ojalá que llueva
> ojalá que llueva café en el campo[1]

So that in this world there wouldn't be
so much suffering,
Oh that it would rain coffee all across the field!
So that all children would sing this song,
Oh that it would rain coffee all across the field!
Oh! How I hope it rains, how I hope it rains!
Oh that it would rain coffee all across the field!

La Despedida: A Reflection of an Intimate Friendship

by David Ham

A Big Heart

While contemplating what to write in this afterword, I was driving around in my car and listening to some old-school hip-hop from the group Truce, a ministry of Nicky Cruz Outreach. Rich used to be one of the rappers in that group, along with a few other guys with whom some of you might be familiar, such as Alex Medina and Andy Mineo. Today, Alex and Andy continue to create music that's reaching the world. But back then—and still today—Rich Pérez *got barz!* If you asked me about my favorite rappers, Rich Pérez is still on my top-ten list in NYC.

I'll never forget the day Rich auditioned with Alex Medina. I'm pretty sure they were both wearing polo shirts two sizes too big. Both of them were very humble, polite, nearly reluctant to audition, and radical about Christ. We always laugh when I recount my reason for having them join the group. "Rich, you guys had *big hearts* at that audition," I tell them. "I figured we could work on the talent over time." But it really wasn't long before Rich became one of our lead rappers. His passion and willingness to serve in every city to which we traveled affected the lives of many people. The growth in Rich's talent, his love for others, and his leadership within the group were all evidence of a higher calling. In the beginning, his heart passion was bigger than his performance, but isn't that where it should always begin? Psalm 37:4 says, "Take delight in the LORD, and he will give you your heart's desires." Rich has always been full of desire. He's an example of what life looks like when your heart's desires are submitted to the will of God. Rich has a desire to serve the community, preach the gospel, love people, and give to those who are in need.

Wadsworth Avenue

After some time, Truce needed a new spot to rehearse on Saturdays. Rich suggested we use the Washington Heights church in which he had grown up. This would be my first significant activity in the Heights. "Rich, how do I say it in Spanish?" Every week I asked him how to pronounce the lengthy name of the church. He'd give me a big smile and purposely respond with a heavy, Dominican accent, *"Primera Iglesia Bautista Hispana de Manhattan."* Of course, my attempt to duplicate his inflection was always an epic failure.

I can remember several times walking into a bodega with Rich. The Dominican man at the counter would assume I was Hispanic, since I was with Rich. Never did I really understand what the guy at the counter was saying to me in Spanish. But one time I boldly responded, "Gracias, Papa!" I can still picture Rich walking out of the bodega, doubled over with laughter at my awkward attempt to sound authentically Dominican.

This wonderful corner church on Wadsworth became our place of fellowship, discipleship, and ministry development. During this season in Washington Heights, I witnessed Rich changing. He was no longer just a young teenager growing up in the community. A new leader was emerging in New York City, and his sense of responsibility to reach his community for Christ was apparent. He believed that what we spent our time doing each week, preparing to reach the nations, would potentially be his permanent commitment in Washington Heights.

New York versus London

It's the championship game. New York versus London. We're down by a couple of points, but we believe we can win this basketball tournament *'cause we from New York City!* If only I had passed the ball to Rich for that second-to-last shot. Instead, I went for a left-hand scoop layup that barely touched the front of the rim. As I recall, Alex Medina took the last shot in an attempt to tie the game, but it didn't touch anything but air. Why didn't we just give the ball to Rich? He was the *go-to* man. Needless to say, we lost the championship. But we weren't in London to play ball anyway. We were on a five-week mission trip with Nicky Cruz. This was 2006, and knife crime in London was at an all-time high, so we spent most of our time ministering in gang-infested communities. And every day, we told those UK boys and girls about Jesus.

I've worked with a lot of young people over the years, taking them around the world to experience different cultures and international missions. Some have developed a genuine passion to continue traveling and doing world outreach.

Rich, however, seized every opportunity to use travel as the training ground to prepare for the mission at home. He embraced every opportunity to travel, and each experience brought him closer to fulfilling a greater calling to the community that weighed on his heart. I'm reminded of the proverb, "Your home will always be the place for which you feel the deepest affection, no matter where you are." In other words, home is where the heart is.

Please Pray

I was only a few blocks away when Alex Medina called me from the hospital. The tremble in his voice compelled me to pull over for a moment. Rich's mother had passed away. I quickly found parking and made my way up to the waiting room. I had never experienced that kind of grief. The small waiting room was filled with family members holding tightly to one another and crying heavily. The weight of grief and sorrow brought me to tears. I cried with Rich and his family, and then he looked up at me and gently said, "Please pray." To be honest, I was nervous. What do I say? I was trembling at the responsibility of praying for Rich and his family in that difficult time. But the trust that he demonstrated made me realize that I was not just his director, mentor, and friend. Rich looked at me as a family member. His love and trust stirred my faith in the greatest hope during the deepest moment of sorrow. We cried, prayed, cried some more, and put our trust in the comfort of the Holy Spirit. The apostle Paul said, "Rejoice with those who rejoice; weep with those who weep" (Rom. 12:15). We can do this only if we love people the way Christ has called us to love. And to love like this is to know that Christ loves us.

First John 4:9 says, "God's love was revealed among us in this way: God sent his one and only Son into the world so that we might live through him." This is why Rich is so passionate about his community. His affection for the city grows out of his affection for the kingdom of God and the love of God revealed to him. This is how we love one another and, more specifically, how we love our neighbors as ourselves (Mark 12:31). Rich Pérez looks at the city in faith and sees the family of God being drawn together by the love of Jesus. This is how the gospel comes alive in the community.

A Place Called Rest: *Recuéstate y Descansa*

Home Base

He was athletic and with a lot of energy, off-the-wall kind of energy. But he wasn't thrilled about baseball. He enjoyed playing it, but he wasn't crazy about it the way he was of other things. With a Dominican heritage running through his blood, all he heard was that he was destined to play it. But in the end, all he really wanted was to be with his dad. His dad was into sports, baseball especially. He figured he would stick with it. With every hit, and with every catch, he would turn his attention to his dad and with his hands lifted high from uncontrollable excitement he would say, "Papi, did you see that?!" But equally devastated, his head swung low with every strikeout, every missed catch or a missed opportunity to do something greater than the rest of the kids. He was certain his dad was disappointed.

There's something about having your dad around that fills a kid with so much excitement and sometimes with so much pressure. There's something about his being around that drives a kid to do his best. He swings harder, runs faster, and gets dirtier. Some kids who didn't have their fathers bitterly do it to prove they don't need him. Perhaps others do it to grab the attention of any older dude watching them. He thinks to himself, *Is he watching? Does he love me? Am I worth the glance? Does he even care?* But what if he knew, in a way that couldn't be shaken, that he stood right at the center of his dad's affections? What if he knew that his achievements could only make his dad proud, but they couldn't make him love his son more or less than he did in that very moment? What if he knew that his father loved him simply because he's his son?

He stood at the plate, staring down the pitcher. It was perhaps the perfect baseball scenario. The one every kid imagined himself in: three balls, two strikes, runners on second and third, down one run. A single down the overlooked and lonely third-base line would win the game. Keeping his eyes on the pitcher, my son raised his hand to the umpire and called for time. Every parent watching was slowly losing weight from both the heat of the day and the stress of the moment. He walked over to me. (I was volunteer coaching the team.) "Dad, I'm nervous," he said to me. "Keep your eye on the ball and you'll be alright, buddy. You got this!" It's all that came out of my mouth. He went back to the plate and the rest of the game happened in slow motion. At least it felt that way. The ball came in, my son had the perfect form and swing, but it seemed like his bat had a gaping hole in it. He swung. He missed. They lost. Eight-year-olds don't make it any easier. The other team ran and cheered, and our team just stared as they celebrated.

Josiah was devastated. He came over to me crying, and after they shook hands with the other team, he said, "I'm sorry, Papi. I'm really sorry." As an athlete and as a dad, I tried my best to understand the pain of losing and perhaps show him that this was part of growing to be a better competitor. But I realized that this was more than just the pain of losing. It seemed deeper; more significant.

"Why are you sorry, buddy?" I asked.

Through tears he said, "I had the chance to win the game and I struck out. You told me to look at the ball and maybe I didn't look at it long enough or closely enough. So . . . I'm sorry."

It was at that moment I realized that my son was perhaps forgetting something incredibly important about our relationship. I asked him, "Jo, do you know why I love you?"

And through his tears, whimpers, and a series of sniffles he said, "I don't know, 'cause I'm cool and stuff."

I chuckled, of course. "Yeah, you're cool, but that's not why I love you. Not even close." That caught his attention. He finally looked up—right into my eyes. "I love you because you're my son."

Perhaps at that moment it didn't all the way register with him where I was going with this. But then I asked him, "When will you stop being my son?" He said, "Umm . . . never." I asked, "So guess what will never change?"

So much of who we are is built around the idea of what we do—our performance. Whatever it may be—a job, a relationship, anything—we often define and appraise ourselves by how well we perform in them. If you do poorly at work, you and often the world around you have a lower appraisal of yourself. Our value—how acceptable we feel, how wanted we feel, etc.—is often tethered to how well we perform. And sure, we can sit here and say that those may be evidences of poor character. Yet we punish ourselves because of failures, inabilities, and bad decisions in ways that God himself doesn't. Instead, God, in the face of our shortcomings, failures, and sins, confronts them and offers freedom from them.

For my son, he believed that my acceptance and love for him was built around how well he could surprise me or make me proud. I would have loved for him to smoke that ball down the left field line, so, sure, the strikeout was disappointing. But the truth is that his achievements and successes only have the power to make me proud. His failures and poor decisions only have the power to disappoint me. But neither have the power to make me love him more or less than I do at any given moment. My love is hinged on the pure reality that he is my son. I am able to love him in success and love him in failure. My love in success is able to celebrate him, his gifting, and remind him in whose hands his achievements are. My love in failure is able to challenge him, draw near to him, and remind him of the power and forgiveness God offers.

I think we could all agree that there's something valuable about occasionally stopping whatever you're doing—or stop wallowing in what you're not doing—and recalling who you are. It's so easy to define yourself by what you do rather than by who you are. Whether you're religious or not, it's always a risky thing to understand yourself based on what you do. The moment you stop doing those things, regardless of the reason, you run the risk of an identity crisis. Life is primarily about discovering who you are, and I am learning that what we do is the result of who we are. Knowing who you are, in relation to God, will result in discovering how he has made you—your gifts, skills, and passions.

Rest Stops

From my adolescent years until I graduated from high school, our family would often take trips down to Atlantic City—or "Atlahntee Seedee," as my Dominican parents would say. We had family down there, so we'd spend a handful of days there during the summers. Along the way, we'd always hit certain stops on I-95 South: the gas station in Elizabeth, New Jersey, near exit 13A, and the McDonalds with the enormous parking lot near exit 2. We stopped to stretch, run, and grab some food. It also gave the parents an opportunity to remind us kids that this seemingly never-ending ride—actually only two hours!—was almost over, and that we would soon see our cousins. Thank goodness we stopped! Those reminders helped keep us crazy kids from losing our minds and making the trip miserable for the adults.

This is exactly what we need as we travel through life. We need to be reminded who we are invited to be in Jesus. These reminders are especially important for those of us who live in fast-paced environments and typically give ourselves to our work. Identity determines activity, so it's important for us to have a healthy understanding of our identity.

Over and over, in both the Bible and my own life experiences, God has always kindly extended various invitations to me. Matthew 11:28 contains one of those invitations: "Come to me, all of you who are weary and burdened, and I will give you rest." Although we don't see it explicitly in this verse, the context paints the whole picture. God is offering us an identity of rest. God is saying that we can be rested people, despite the realities of a hustle-and-bustle city culture that often appraises us by what we can and cannot do. But the church doesn't fall far behind. Those of us in the church, sadly, also sometimes define and appraise people by what they can do or how they can contribute to our agenda. But God calls us to see faith and grace as the means to bring us into intimate and meaningful relationship with God. Nothing else.

Whether it's our culture's rhythms, our families' hopes for us, the demands of our jobs, or even our own insecurities, there are things that we all want to find a way past. There is always that moment, often at the midpoint of your day, when you cannot wait to plop yourself into your bed, go to sleep, and not think about anything. The truth is that there are nights when we cannot fall asleep, despite being exhausted, for thinking about things we left undone or that are waiting for us the next day. It seems like life, unsupervised by rest, feels more like death.

"God, as our bodies rest on our beds, may our hearts rest on your promises. Amen." That's how we pray every night—at least we try to pray every night—with our kids. The simple truth behind this closing prayer is that just as our bodies need rest, so do our hearts. We'll rest our bodies on anything from a plush, good-for-your-back, overnight-magic-working mattress to one of those good-for-nothing, never-stay-inflated air mattresses! Similarly, we'll either rest our identity on something able to sustain it, or we won't. Our hearts can be worn down by the thorny rhythms and expectations of life, and my ability to be joyful is often forfeited because of those rhythms. Consider Hebrews 3 and 4. It's inspired by Israel's experience coming out of Egypt, just before entering the land that God had promised them through Abraham back in Genesis 12. You have an oppressed people, who are in constant fear of their lives, in constant pressure from their work and disillusioned with their traditions. God brought the people out from under the oppression they experienced in Egypt and promised them a land with abundant provision and complete security. In other words, God is saying, "I'm going to free you and bring you to a place where you will have all that you need and more; and even more than that, you will feel completely safe and protected."

But something happened between here and there that resulted in many of them not entering that place. If you notice Hebrews 4:2, 6, the author says, "For we also have received the good news just as they did. But the message they heard did not benefit them, since they were not united with those who heard it in faith." And then he says again, "those who formerly received the good news did not enter because of disobedience . . ."

You see historically, between Egypt and the land that God promised is a place where God's people spent forty years—the wilderness, literally translated, "chaos." Between the oppressed place that God takes you out of and the place of perfect rest is this strange and chaotic place, where the only thing that will help you not merely survive the journey but thrive in it is God himself.

I'm only now coming to understand how demanding living in an urban center like New York is. It has been significantly important for our family to learn rest. Here are a few ways we've come to understand rest:

Rest Is a Sign

If you're a person who drives often, you're probably thinking of a road sign. Say you're driving up the Westside Highway and see a sign that reads "Dyckman. Turn right in 800 ft." That sign is there to tell you that your exit is approaching; that something is coming in the near future—so be aware! Although that is a sign, that's not quite the sign I'm talking about here. I believe that the kind of sign I'm talking about is more like what *chamaquitos* in the 'hood do when the street is freshly poured. They "tag" it! "Rich was here!"

A conversation between God and Moses in Exodus 31 sheds some light to this:

> The LORD said to Moses: "Tell the Israelites: You must observe my Sabbaths, for it is a sign between me and you throughout your generations, so that you will know that I am the LORD who consecrates you. Observe the Sabbath, for it is holy for you. Whoever profanes it must be put to death. If anyone does work on it, that person must be cut off from his people." (vv. 12–14)

Just as it was to God's people in Exodus, the Sabbath-Rest is a sign of a relationship between God and his people that utterly depended and continues to depend on God to sustain. Now, take notice of verse 13: "for it is a sign between me and you throughout your generations, so that you will know that I am the LORD who consecrates you."

This is perhaps one of the most difficult things for us to admit: our limitations. Whether we say this with our words or not, our actions make it clear. The word *sanctify* is translated, "to be set apart as holy," or in other words, to be made like God. God is the only being purely good and purely set aside from anyone else. Rest is to remember our brokenness, God's wholeness, and the relationship between the two.

The Satisfactions of Rest

If there is anything I see as a common thread in American culture, especially in global cities like ours, it is this—a deep dissatisfaction with our present realities. When the New York City Comptroller tells me that New Yorkers spend the most hours at work than anyone else in the country by eight hours per week, I see dissatisfaction. When the APA (American Psychological Association) tells me that nearly half of marriages end in divorce, I hear dissatisfaction. When the University of Chicago tells me that a third of the American population is generally unhappy with their life, I see dissatisfaction. When the *Wall Street Journal* tells me that nearly 51 percent of people change work or careers once every four years, I see dissatisfaction. Why do we work long hours? Why do we change careers as often as we do? Why are marriages and families becoming an invisible demographic in cities like ours?

It seems that just like the Israelites in the wilderness, we, too, are clouded and discouraged by the responsibilities *on* us, the expectations *of* us, the difficulties *against* us, and the insecurities *in* us.

Something interesting happens in our Hebrews passage. On two occasions, the author alludes to the creation story of Genesis in connection to rest: "For somewhere he has spoken about the seventh day in this way: "And on the seventh day God rested from all his works" (Heb. 4:4). And then he says, "For the person who has entered [God's] rest has rested from his own works, just as God did from his" (v. 10).

And then notice the remainder of Exodus 31 that we didn't read before, "Work may be done for six days, but on the seventh day there must be a Sabbath of complete rest, holy to the LORD. Anyone who does work on the Sabbath day must be put to death. The Israelites must observe the Sabbath, celebrating it throughout their generations as a permanent covenant. It is a sign forever between me and the Israelites, for in six days the LORD made the heavens and the earth, but on the seventh day he rested and was refreshed" (vv. 15–17).

Why does the author mention God resting after his work? Was God tired? Did he need a break? Absolutely not. That's not why he rested. If we look closely, Genesis tells us why he took a Sabbath.

God took Sabbath because of Genesis 1:31–2:1: "God saw all that he had made, and it was very good indeed. . . . So the heavens and the earth and everything in them were completed."

God rested not because he was tired, but because his work was done and now it was time to enjoy it! Rest, as God offers it, is to live a lifestyle fueled by the greatness of God's presence and his work in our world. To rest means to trust God when he says, through the prophet Isaiah: "Remember this and stand firm, recall it to mind, you transgressors, remember the former things of old; for I am God, and there is no other; I am God, and there is none like me" (Isa. 46:8–9 ESV). If you live a life that avoids faithful rest, you begin to believe quite the opposite of what Isaiah is saying to us here. To avoid rest is to avoid this truth. Instead of "You are God alone and there is no other, you are God alone and there is none like you," we instead say, "I am God alone and I can't afford time off because it all depends on me!"

The reality of gospel rest comes to a head in Luke 6:1–6, where the Bible describes:

> On a Sabbath, he passed through the grainfields. His disciples were picking heads of grain, rubbing them in their hands, and eating them. But some of the Pharisees said, "Why are you doing what is not lawful on the Sabbath?"
>
> Jesus answered them, "Haven't you read what David and those who were with him

did when he was hungry—how he entered the house of God and took and ate the bread of the Presence, which is not lawful for any but the priests to eat? He even gave some to those who were with him."
Then he told them, "The Son of Man is Lord of the Sabbath."

Jesus demonstrates that he is the master over the Sabbath-Rest when he willingly gives his life as a sacrifice for humanity Friday at sundown and raises from the dead Sunday at sunrise. Doesn't it seem interesting that Jesus would die on the Jewish Sabbath? They even hurried along his death and burial. "Since it was the preparation day, the Jews did not want the bodies to remain on the cross on the Sabbath (for that Sabbath was a special day). They requested that Pilate have the men's legs broken and that their bodies be taken away" (John 19:31). The Jews didn't even want to have to think about taking down his body and burying him after Sabbath. They just wanted to be done with him. And according to the Jewish law anyone hanged on a tree was cursed. The Jews didn't even want to run the risk of cursing the land by leaving Jesus and the other criminals hanging on the tree overnight. They just wanted to end this "messiah looney" chapter and go home, and in their zeal, offer prayers and traditions to God that they hoped would clear them before him. The irony! While everyone "rested" on the day of Sabbath, Jesus *worked* against death for our salvation.

There is no doubt that the Sabbath, as God intended it, gives room for Jesus to work on our behalf. And this allows for us to have a way to *rest* our hearts and lives on that work for us. It allows for us to operate from a deeper sense of patience, faith, and justice. Patience, because in our rest we grow deeply familiar with God and his patience toward us. If we live our lives believing that it all depends on us, then we simply don't have time for anyone else. Faith because in our rest we grow deeply familiar with the presence of God himself through the Holy Spirit. It serves as a kind of faith that, despite great darkness and difficulty, impels you by the overpowering presence of God in your life. Justice because in our rest we've come to see the injustice of sin that has caused pain in your life and in the lives around you, God has confronted your darkness and reconciled your relationship with him. You are now compelled to seek justice in your own relationships and the justice of the world around.

Notes

Introduction

1. *In the Heights* (Original Cast), "When You're Home," Ghostlight, 2008.
2. Juan Luis Guerra, "Visa Para un Sueño," *Ojalá Que Llueva Café,* EMI Music, 1989.
3. G. K. Chesterton, *Orthodoxy* (North Charleston, NC: Createspace, 2009), 34–35.
4. Justin Buzzard and Stephen T. Um, *Why Cities Matter* (Wheaton, IL: Crossway, 2013), 34–35.

Chapter 1

1. Rosanne Cash, "New York, in the Mirror" in *Never Can Say Goodbye: Writers on Their Unshakable Love for New York* by Sari Botton (New York, NY: Touchstone Books, 2014), 4.
2. Casey Gerald, "Purpose Is the New Bottom Line," Lecture, Revolution, New York, NY, June 27, 2015.
3. Tatiana Schlossberg, "Bodegas Declining in Manhattan as Rents Rise and Chains Grow," *New York Times,* August 3, 2015. Internet.
4. Ibid.

5. *In the Heights* (Original Cast), "Finale," Ghostlight, 2008. *In the Heights* by Lin-Manuel (Broadway; New York, NY).

6. Abraham Cho, "Why Race Matters to God and What That Means for Us," Lecture, Redeemer East Side (New York, NY).

7. "Letter from Birmingham Jail," Letter from Martin Luther King Jr. April 16, 1963, in *Gospel of Freedom: Martin Luther King Jr.'s Letter from Birmingham Jail and the Struggle That Changed a Nation* (London, UK: Bloomsbury Press, 2014).

8. Juan Martinez, "Outside the Gates: Evangelicalism and Latino Protestant Theology." Lecture, Theology Conference 2011: Global Theology in Evangelical Perspective (Wheaton College, Wheaton, IL).

Chapter 2

1. *New York: A Documentary Film*, directed by Ric Burns (New York, NY: Steeplechase Productions, 1999).

2. Ibid.

3. Woody Allen, "Examining Psychic Phenomena," *The New Yorker* (New York, NY), October 7, 1972.

4. "Number of Homeless People in NYC Shelters Each Night," Coalition for the Homeless, September 2011. Accessed January 4, 2015. http://www.coalitionforthehomeless.org/the-catastrophe-of-homelessness/facts-about-homelessness/.

5. *On the Map: The Atlas of Family Homelessness in New York City*, Report, October 2014, http://www.icphusa.org

/PDF/reports/OnTheMap_TheAtlasofFamilyHomelessness
inNewYorkCity.pdf.

6. Ibid.

7. Ibid.

8. Justo L. González, *Mañana: Christian Theology from a Hispanic Perspective* (Nashville, TN: Abingdon Press, 1990), 41.

9. Justo González, *Santa Biblia: The Bible Through Hispanic Eyes* (Nashville, TN: Abingdon Press, 1996), 80.

10. Virgilio Elizondo, *Galilean Journey: The Mexican-American Promise* (Maryknoll, NY: Orbis Books, 2000),18.

Chapter 3

1. Rebecca Manley Pippert, "The 'Heresy' of Niceness," Lecture, Principles TV: Precepts of Leadership, January 4, 2015, https://www.youtube.com/watch?v=xZS6SLI63sM.

2. *The Fresh Prince of Bel-Air*, "Papa's Got a Brand New Excuse," directed by Shelley Jensen, aired May 9, 1994.

3. Justo L. González, "Violence and Love," MACC: Empowering and Educating a Culturally Diverse Church, February 9, 2012.

Chapter 4

1. Juan Luis Guerra, *Ojalá Que Llueva Café*, 1989, CD.